PELICAN BOOKS

Advisory Editors: H. L. BEALES, Reader in Economic History, University of London; W. E. WILLIAMS, Secretary, the British Institute of Adult Education.

Ann Davies.

THE CENTURY'S POETRY
1837–1937

AN ANTHOLOGY COMPILED BY
DENYS KILHAM ROBERTS

VOL. 1
HOOD TO HARDY

PELICAN BOOKS

THE CENTURY'S POETRY
1837–1937

AN ANTHOLOGY COMPILED BY DENYS KILHAM ROBERTS

VOL. 1
HOOD TO HARDY

PUBLISHED BY
PENGUIN BOOKS LIMITED
HARMONDSWORTH MIDDLESEX ENGLAND
41 EAST 28TH STREET NEW YORK U.S.A.

First Published (Pelican Books) 1938
Reprinted 1940

MADE AND PRINTED IN GREAT BRITAIN BY
HAZELL, WATSON & VINEY, LTD., LONDON AND AYLESBURY

PREFACE

IN compiling this two-volume anthology of the Century's poetry I have set out as far as possible to forget the existence of other anthologies and by a new examination of the whole of a poet's work to reassess its value and importance from the viewpoint of the present generation; when, however, my choices have coincided with those of other anthologists I have not, merely to be different, substituted a poem that I liked less well. We are all inclined to have our judgment of certain poems blurred by a familiarity for which our school-days, coupled with the *Golden Treasury* and the *Oxford Book of Verse*, are mainly responsible, and, just as it is difficult for most sons and daughters to take an objective critical view of their parents, so it is difficult for the student or reader of poetry to take an objective critical view of the poems he knows by heart, especially if they are poems he learnt in childhood when, owing to inexperience, his critical faculty could not be sufficiently developed to enable him to judge of their merit. Some heavily anthologised poems are included in the present collection; many are omitted; but I cannot pretend that in every instance I have been able to achieve the degree of objectiveness required or that I have always succeeded in severing a familiar poem from its personal associations.

Sentimentality; banality; pretentiousness; insincerity; imitativeness; jingoism and jingleism; triteness and conventionality of idea, imagery and phrasing; and, above all, poetics, I have ruthlessly barred from admission except in cases in which there seemed to me to be redeeming features which more than compensate.

The anthology is designed to include the work of such poets who were living in 1837 and such poets who have been born since as in my view have had something not only worth saying but worth repeating and have expressed what they had to say better than anyone else has been able to express it. The anthology should, if I had slavishly followed this plan, have begun with Wordsworth who physically survived Victoria's accession by thirteen years, but since Wordsworth the poet died thirty years before Wordsworth the man I decided to omit him and to start with Hood.

The question of order is always one of the anthologist's most embarrassing problems. He may, as Palgrave did, arrange his compilation according to personal whim, but this is a policy which can only be commended if people are going to read the book through page by page as if it were a novel. I don't believe one person in a hundred reads an anthology in this way, and as it is obvious that the customary alternative of placing poets in the order of their birthdates may often be misleading I have in this collection placed the poets in an order based upon the date which marks the middle of their adult lives. This is not a perfect solution of the difficulty, but unless every poem is to be entered under the year in which it was written, it must give a truer idea than most others of the course poetry has followed for the past hundred years.

Several poets are omitted or represented less fully than I would have wished owing to copyright difficulties or, in the case of the second volume, owing to the not unreasonable refusal of certain living poets to permit examples of their work to be removed from their context. In general, however, I have been fortunate in receiving the most cordial cooperation from the poets themselves or, when the poets are no longer living, from their publishers and representatives.

D. K. R.

ACKNOWLEDGEMENTS

I MUST thank the following for permission to include copyright poems in Volume I: The Oxford University Press and the Poet's Family for the poems by Gerard Manley Hopkins; Mr. Leicester-Warren for the poems by Lord de Tabley; the Author's Executors for the poem by Dr. Richard Garnett; the Trustees of Oscar Wilde and Messrs. Parker, Garrett & Co. for the poem by Oscar Wilde; Messrs. G. Bell & Sons for the poems by Coventry Patmore; Sir Henry Newbolt for the poem by Mary Coleridge; Messrs. Macmillan for the poems by W. E. Henley, Wilfrid Scawen Blunt and Thomas Hardy; Messrs. Heinemann for the poems by Algernon Charles Swinburne; the Trustees of George Meredith and Messrs. Constable for the poems by George Meredith; Messrs. Longmans for the poem by William Bell Scott; Mr. Lloyd Osbourne for the poems by R. L. Stevenson; the Author's Widow and Mr. Grant Richards for John Davidson's *The Last Journey*; Messrs. John Lane The Bodley Head for the other poem by John Davidson and the poem by Ernest Dowson.

D. K. R.

CONTENTS

9

AUTUMN

Thomas Hood

I saw old Autumn in the misty morn
Stand shadowless like Silence, listening
To silence, for no lonely bird would sing
Into his hollow ear from woods forlorn,
Nor lowly hedge nor solitary thorn;
Shaking his languid locks all dewy bright
With tangled gossamer that fell by night,
   Pearling his coronet of golden corn.

Where are the songs of Summer?—With the sun,
Oping the dusky eyelids of the south,
Till shade and silence waken up as one,
And Morning sings with a warm odorous
    mouth.
Where are the merry birds?—Away, away,
On panting wings through the inclement skies,
     Lest owls should prey
      Undazzled at noonday,
And tear with horny beak their lustrous eyes.

Where are the blooms of Summer?—In the
    west,
Blushing their last to the last sunny hours,
When the mild Eve by sudden Night is prest
Like tearful Proserpine, snatched from her
    flowers
     To a most gloomy breast.
Where is the pride of Summer,—the green
    prime,—
The many, many leaves all twinkling?—Three
On the mossed elm; three on the naked lime
Trembling,—and one upon the old oak tree!

Thomas
Hood   Where is the Dryads' immortality?—
Gone into mournful cypress and dark yew,
Or wearing the long gloomy Winter through
    In the smooth holly's green eternity.

The squirrel gloats on his accomplished hoard,
The ants have brimmed their garners with ripe
        grain,
            And honey bees have stored
The sweets of Summer in their luscious cells;
The swallows all have winged across the main;
But here the Autumn melancholy dwells,
And sighs her tearful spells,
Amongst the sunless shadows of the plain.
        Alone, alone,
            Upon a mossy stone,
She sits and reckons up the dead and gone
With the last leaves for a love-rosary,
Whilst all the withered world looks drearily,
Like a dim picture of the drowned past
In the hushed mind's mysterious far away,
Doubtful what ghostly thing will steal the last
Into that distance, grey upon the grey.

O go and sit with her, and be o'ershaded
Under the languid downfall of her hair:
She wears a coronal of flowers faded
Upon her forehead, and a face of care;
There is enough of withered everywhere
To make her bower,—and enough of gloom;
There is enough of sadness to invite,
If only for the rose that died,—whose doom
Is Beauty's,—she that with the living bloom
Of conscious cheeks most beautifies the light:

There is enough of sorrowing, and quite
Enough of bitter fruits the earth doth bear,—
Enough of chilly droppings for her bowl;
Enough of fear and shadowy despair,
To frame her cloudy prison for the soul !

Thomas Hood

BALLAD

It was not in the winter
　　Our loving lot was cast !
It was the time of roses,
　　We plucked them as we passed !

That churlish season never frowned
　　On early lovers yet !
Oh no—the world was newly crowned
　　With flowers, when first we met !

'Twas twilight, and I bade you go,
　　But still you held me fast;
It was the time of roses,
　　We plucked them as we passed !

What else could peer my glowing cheek
　　That tears began to stud ?
And when I asked the like of Love
　　You snatched a damask bud,—

And oped it to the dainty core
　　Still glowing to the last:
It was the time of roses,
　　We plucked them as we passed !

THE BROKEN DISH

What's life but full of care and doubt,
    With all its fine humanities;
With parasols we walk about,
    Long pigtails and such vanities.

We plant pomegranate trees and things,
    And go in gardens sporting,
With toys and fans of peacocks' wings,
    To painted ladies courting.

We gather flowers of every hue,
    And fish in boats for fishes,
Build summer-houses painted blue,—
    But life's as frail as dishes.

Walking about their groves of trees,
    Blue bridges and blue rivers,
How little thought them two Chinese
    They'd both be smashed to shivers.

THE BRIDGE OF SIGHS

One more unfortunate,
Weary of breath,
Rashly importunate,
Gone to her death!

Take her up tenderly,
Lift her with care;
Fashioned so slenderly,
Young, and so fair!

16

Look at her garments   *Thomas*
Clinging like cerements   *Hood*
Whilst the wave constantly
Drips from her clothing;
Take her up instantly,
Loving, not loathing.

Touch her not scornfully;
Think of her mournfully,
Gently and humanly;
Not of the stains of her;
All that remains of her
Now is pure womanly.

Make no deep scrutiny
Into her mutiny
Rash and undutiful;
Past all dishonour,
Death has left on her
Only the beautiful.

Still, for all slips of hers,
One of Eve's family—
Wipe those poor lips of hers,
Oozing so clammily.

Loop up her tresses
Escaped from the comb,
Her fair auburn tresses;
Whilst wonderment guesses
Where was her home?

Who was her father?
Who was her mother?

Thomas
Hood

Had she a sister ?
Had she a brother ?
Or was there a dearer one
Still, and a nearer one
Yet, than all other ?

Alas ! for the rarity
Of Christian charity
Under the sun !
Oh ! it was pitiful !
Near a whole city full,
Home she had none !

Sisterly, brotherly,
Fatherly, motherly
Feelings had changed :
Love, by harsh evidence,
Thrown from its eminence ;
Even God's providence
Seeming estranged.

Where the lamps quiver
So far in the river,
With many a light
From window and casement,
From garret to basement,
She stood, with amazement,
Houseless by night.

The bleak wind of March
Made her tremble and shiver ;
But not the dark arch,
Or the black flowing river.

Mad from life's history,
Glad to death's mystery,
Swift to be hurled—
Anywhere, anywhere,
Out of the world !

*Thomas
Hood*

In she plunged boldly,
No matter how coldly
The rough river ran,—
Over the brink of it,
Picture it—think of it,
Dissolute Man !
Lave in it, drink of it,
Then, if you can !

Take her up tenderly,
Lift her with care;
Fashioned so slenderly,
Young, and so fair !

Ere her limbs frigidly
Stiffen too rigidly,
Decently, kindly,
Smooth and compose them.
And her eyes, close them,
Staring so blindly !

Dreadfully staring
Through muddy impurity,
As when with the daring
Last look of despairing
Fixed on futurity.

Perishing gloomily,
Spurred by contumely,
Cold inhumanity,
Burning insanity
Into her rest.
Cross her hands humbly,
As if praying dumbly,
Over her breast!

Owning her weakness,
Her evil behaviour,
And leaving, with meekness,
Her sins to her Saviour!

SILENCE

There is a silence where hath been no sound,
There is a silence where no sound may be,
In the cold grave—under the deep, deep sea,
Or in wide desert where no life is found,
Which hath been mute, and still must sleep
     profound;
No voice is hushed—no life treads silently,
But clouds and cloudy shadows wander free,
That never spoke, over the idle ground:
But in green ruins, in the desolate walls
Of antique palaces, where Man hath been,
Though the dun fox, or wild hyena, calls,
And owls, that flit continually between,
Shriek to the echo, and the low winds moan,
There the true Silence is, self-conscious and
     alone.

"IT IS NOT DEATH"

Thomas Hood

It is not death, that sometime in a sigh
This eloquent breath shall take its speechless
  flight;
That sometime these bright stars, that now
  reply
In sunlight to the sun, shall set in night;
That this warm conscious flesh shall perish
  quite,
And all life's ruddy springs forget to flow;
That thoughts shall cease, and the immortal
  sprite
Be lapped in alien clay and laid below;
It is not death to know this,—but to know
That pious thoughts, which visit at new graves
In tender pilgrimage, will cease to go
So duly and so oft,—and when grass waves
Over the passed-away, there may be then
No resurrection in the minds of men.

RONDEAU

Leigh Hunt

Jenny kissed me when we met,
  Jumping from the chair she sat in;
Time, you thief, who love to get
  Sweets into your list, put that in!
Say I'm weary, say I'm sad
  Say that health and wealth have missed me,
Say I'm growing old, but add,
      Jenny kissed me.

We are the Fairies, blithe and antic,
Of dimensions not gigantic,
Though the moonshine mostly keep us,
Oft in orchards frisk and peep us.

Stolen sweets are always sweeter,
Stolen kisses much completer,
Stolen looks are nice in chapels,
Stolen, stolen be your apples !

When to bed the world are bobbing,
Then's the time for orchard robbing;
Yet the fruit were scarce worth peeling
Were it not for stealing, stealing.

THE NILE

It flows through old hushed Egypt and its sands,
Like some grave mighty thought threading a
    dream,
And times and things, as in that vision, seem
Keeping along in their eternal stands,—
Caves, pillars, pyramids, the shepherd bands
That roamed through the young earth, the glory
    extreme
Of high Sesostris, and that southern beam,
The laughing queen that caught the world's
    great hands.

Then comes a mightier silence, stern and strong, *Leigh*
As of a world left empty of its throng, *Hunt*
And the void weighs on us; and then we wake,
And hear the fruitful stream lapsing along
'Twixt villages, and think how we shall take
Our own calm journey on for human sake.

TO A FRIEND

*Hartley
Coleridge*

When we were idlers with the loitering rills,
The need of human love we little noted:
Our love was nature; and the peace that floated
On the white mist, and dwelt upon the hills,
To sweet accord subdued our wayward wills:
One soul was ours, one mind, one heart devoted,
That, wisely doating, asked not why it doated,
And ours the unknown joy, which knowing kills.
But now I find, how dear thou wert to me;
That man is more than half of nature's treasure,
Of that fair Beauty which no eye can see,
Of that sweet music which no ear can measure;
And now the streams may sing for others'
    pleasure,
The hills sleep on in their eternity.

LIBERTY

Say, What is Freedom? What the right of souls
Which all who know are bound to keep, or die,
And who knows not, is dead? In vain ye pry
In musty archives, or retentive scrolls,
Charters and statutes, constitutions, rolls,

23

And remnants of the old world's history:—
These show what has been, not what ought to be,
Or teach at best how wiser Time controls
Man's futile purposes.   As vain the search
Of restless factions, who, in lawless will,
Fix the foundations of a creedless church—
A lawless rule—an anarchy of ill:
But what is Freedom?   Rightly understood,
A universal license to be good.

"IS LOVE A FANCY"

Is love a fancy, or a feeling?   No,
It is immortal as immaculate Truth.
'Tis not a blossom, shed as soon as youth
Drops from the stem of life—for it will grow
In barren regions, where no waters flow,
Nor ray of promise cheats the pensive gloom.
A darkling fire, faint hovering o'er a tomb,
That but itself and darkness nought doth shew,
Is my love's being,—yet it cannot die,
Nor will it change, though all be changed beside;
Though fairest beauty be no longer fair,
Though vows be false, and faith itself deny,
Though sharp enjoyment be a suicide,
And hope a spectre in a ruin bare.

"LONG TIME A CHILD . . ."

Long time a child, and still a child, when years
Had painted manhood on my cheek, was I,—
For yet I lived like one not born to die;

24

A thriftless prodigal of smiles and tears, *Hartley*
No hope I needed, and I knew no fears. *Coleridge*
But sleep, though sweet, is only sleep, and
    waking,
I waked to sleep no more, at once o'ertaking
The vanguard of my age, with all arrears
Of duty on my back.　Nor child, nor man,
Nor youth, nor sage, I find my head is grey,
For I have lost the race I never ran:
A rathe December blights my lagging May;
And still I am a child, though I be old,
Time is my debtor for my years untold.

THE WAR SONG OF DINAS FAWR

Thomas Love Peacock

  The mountain sheep are sweeter,
  But the valley sheep are fatter;
  We therefore deemed it meeter
  To carry off the latter.
  We made an expedition;
  We met a host, and quelled it;
  We forced a strong position,
  And killed the men who held it.

  On Dyfed's richest valley,
  Where herds of kine were browsing,
  We made a mighty sally,
  To furnish our carousing.
  Fierce warriors rushed to meet us;
  We met them, and o'erthrew them:
  They struggled hard to beat us;
  But we conquered them, and slew them.

As we drove our prize at leisure,
The king marched forth to catch us:
His rage surpassed all measure,
But his people could not match us.
He fled to his hall-pillars;
And, ere our force we led off,
Some sacked his house and cellars,
While others cut his head off.

We there, in strife bewildering,
Spilt blood enough to swim in:
We orphaned many children,
And widowed many women.
The eagles and the ravens
We glutted with our foemen;
The heroes and the cravens,
The spearmen and the bowmen.

We brought away from battle,
And much their land bemoaned them,
Two thousand head of cattle,
And the head of him who owned them:
Ednyfed, King of Dyfed,
His head was borne before us;
His wine and beasts supplied our feasts,
And his overthrow, our chorus.

THREE MEN OF GOTHAM

Seamen three ! What men be ye ?
Gotham's three wise men we be.
Whither in your bowl so free ?
To rake the moon from out the sea.

The bowl goes trim.   The moon doth shine.   *Thomas*
And our ballast is old wine.—   *Love*
And your ballast is old wine.   *Peacock*

Who art thou, so fast adrift ?
I am he they call Old Care.
Here on board we will thee lift.
No : I may not enter there.
Wherefore so ?   'Tis Jove's decree,
In a bowl Care may not be.—
In a bowl Care may not be.

Fear ye not the waves that roll ?
No : in charmèd bowl we swim.
What the charm that floats the bowl ?
Water may not pass the brim.
The bowl goes trim.   The moon doth shine.
And our ballast is old wine.—
And your ballast is old wine.

DIRGE   *Thomas*
From DEATH'S JEST-BOOK   *Lovell*
                               Beddoes

If thou wilt ease thine heart
Of love and all its smart,
     Then sleep, dear, sleep ;
And not a sorrow
   Hang any tear on your eyelashes ;
     Lie still and deep,
   Sad soul, until the sea-wave washes
The rim o' the sun to-morrow,
     In eastern sky.

But wilt thou cure thine heart
Of love and all its smart,
    Then die, dear, die;
'Tis deeper, sweeter,
    Than on a rose-bank to lie dreaming
      With folded eye;
    And there alone, amid the beaming
Of love's stars, thou'lt meet her
      In eastern sky.

SPEECH BY ISBRAND
From DEATH'S JEST-BOOK

Then go where Pride and Madness carry thee:
And let that feasted fatness pine and shrink,
Till thy ghost's pinched in the tight love-lean
    body.
I see his life, as in a map of rivers,
Through shadows, over rocks, breaking its way,
Until it meet his brother's, and with that
Wrestle and tumble o'er a perilous rock,
Bare as Death's shoulder: one of them is lost,
And a dark haunted flood creeps deadly on
Into the wailing Styx.   Poor Amala !
A thorny rose thy life is, plucked in the dew,
And pitilessly woven with these snakes
Into a garland for the King of the grave.

SONG
From DEATH'S JEST-BOOK

Old Adam, the carrion crow,
  The old crow of Cairo;
He sat in the shower, and let it flow

28

Under his tail and over his crest; *Thomas*
  And through every feather *Lovell*
  Leaked the wet weather; *Beddoes*
And the bough swung under his nest;
For his beak it was heavy with marrow.
  Is that the wind dying? O no;
  It's only two devils, that blow
  Through a murderer's bones, to and fro,
  In the ghosts' moonshine.

Ho! Eve, my grey carrion wife,
  When we have supped on kings' marrow,
Where shall we drink and make merry our life?
  Our nest it is Queen Cleopatra's skull,
   'Tis cloven and cracked,
   And battered and hacked,
But with tears of blue eyes it is full:
Let us drink then, my raven of Cairo!
  Is that the wind dying? O no;
  It's only two devils, that blow
  Through a murderer's bones, to and fro,
  In the ghosts' moonshine.

SPEECH BY VERONICA
From TORRISMOND

    Who's there? I dreamt:
As I do love that broad, smooth-edged star,
And her young, vandyked moons that climb the
    night
Round their faint mother, I would not have had
Another eye peeping upon that dream,
For one of them to wear upon my breast;

29

Thomas
Lovell
Beddoes And I'll not whisper it, for fear these flags
Should chance to be the green posterity
Of that eaves-dropping, woman-witted grass,
That robbed the snoring wasps of their least
      voice,
To teach their feathery gossips of the air
What long and furry ears king Midas sprouted;
And I'll not think of it, for meditation
Oft presses from the heart its inmost wish,
And thaws its silence into straying words.

SPEECH BY DUKE
From TORRISMOND

        I never was unjust, but when I pardoned
Your bloody sins and ravening appetites—
For which Heaven pardon me, as I repent it !
But I'll not play at battledore with words.
Hear me, young man, in whom I did express
The venom of my nature, thus the son,
Not of my virtuous will, but foul desires;
Not of my life, but of a wicked moment;
Not of my soul, but growing from my body,
Like thorns or poison on a wholesome tree,
The rank excrescence of my tumid sins—
And so I tear thee off: for, Heaven doth know,
All gentler remedies I have applied;
But to this head thy rankling vice has swelled,
That, if thou dwellest in my bosom longer,
Thou wilt infect my blood, corrode my heart,
And blight my being: therefore, off for ever !

SOLILOQUY BY ORAZIO
From PRISON THOUGHTS

Thomas Lovell Beddoes

    I'll speak again:
This rocky wall's great silence frightens me,
Like a dead giant's.
Methought I heard a sound; but all is still.
This empty silence is so deadly low,
The very stir and winging of my thoughts
Make audible my being: every sense
Aches from its depth with hunger.
The pulse of time is stopped, and night's blind
    sun
Sheds its black light, the ashes of noon's beams,
On this forgotten tower, whose ugly round,
Amid the fluency of brilliant morn,
Hoops in a blot of parenthetic night,
Like ink upon the crystal page of day,
Crossing its joy ! But now some lamp awakes,
And, with the venom of a basilisk's wink,
Burns the dark winds. Who comes ?

SONG OF THE STYGIAN NAIADES

Proserpine may pull her flowers,
  Wet with dew or wet with tears,
  Red with anger, pale with fears,
Is it any fault of ours,

Thomas If Pluto be an amorous king,
  Lovell   And comes home nightly, laden,
Beddoes Underneath his broad bat-wing,
        With a gentle mortal maiden?
    Is it so, Wind, is it so?
    All that you and I do know
    Is, that we saw fly and fix
    'Mongst the reeds and flowers of Styx,
          Yesterday,
      Where the Furies made their hay
      For a bed of tiger cubs,
      A great fly of Beelzebub's,
      The bee of hearts, which mortals name
      Cupid, Love, and Fie for shame.

    Proserpine may weep in rage,
      But, ere I and you have done
      Kissing, bathing in the sun,
    What I have in yonder cage,
    Bird or serpent, wild or tame,
      She shall guess and ask in vain;
      But, if Pluto does 't again,
    It shall sing out loud his shame.
    What hast caught then?   What hast caught?
    Nothing but a poet's thought,
    Which so light did fall and fix
    'Mongst the reeds and flowers of Styx,
          Yesterday,
      Where the Furies made their hay
      For a bed of tiger cubs,
      A great fly of Beelzebub's,
      The bee of hearts, which mortals name
      Cupid, Love, and Fie for shame.

THE CITY IN THE SEA

*Edgar
Allan
Poe*

Lo !   Death has reared himself a throne
In a strange city lying alone
Far down within the dim West,
Where the good and the bad and the worst and
  the best
Have gone to their eternal rest.
There shrines and palaces and towers
(Time-eaten towers that tremble not)
Resemble nothing that is ours.
Around, by lifting winds forgot,
Resignedly beneath the sky
The melancholy waters lie.

No rays from the holy heaven come down
On the long night-time of that town;
But light from out the lurid sea
Streams up the turrets silently—
Gleams up the pinnacles far and free—
Up domes—up spires—up kingly halls—
Up fanes—up Babylon-like walls—
Up shadowy long-forgotten bowers
Of sculptured ivy and stone flowers—
Up many and many a marvellous shrine
Whose wreathed friezes intertwine
The viol, the violet, and the vine.

Resignedly, beneath the sky
The melancholy waters lie.
So blend the turrets and shadows there
That all seem pendulous in air;

Edgar
Allan
Poe While, from a proud tower in the town,
Death looks gigantically down.

There open fanes and gaping graves
Yawn level with the luminous waves,
But not the riches there that lie
In each idol's diamond eye,—
Not the gayly-jewelled dead
Tempt the waters from their bed;
For no ripples curl, alas !
Along that wilderness of glass;
No swellings tell that winds may be
Upon some far-off happier sea;
No heavings hint that winds have been
On scenes less hideously serene.

But lo ! a stir is in the air !
The wave—there is a movement there !
As if the towers had thrust aside,
In slightly sinking, the dull tide,—
As if their tops had feebly given
A void within the filmy Heaven.
The waves have now a redder glow,
The hours are breathing faint and low;
And when, amid no earthly moans,
Down, down that town shall settle hence,
Hell, rising from a thousand thrones,
Shall do it reverence.

ROMANCE

Edgar
Allan
Poe

Romance, who loves to nod and sing,
With drowsy head and folded wing,
Among the green leaves as they shake
Far down within some shadowy lake,
   To me a painted paroquet
Hath been a most familiar bird,—
   Taught me my alphabet to say—
To lisp my very earliest word
While in the wild wood I did lie,
A child—with a most knowing eye.

Of late, eternal Condor years
   So shake the very Heaven on high
   With tumult as they thunder by,
I have no time for idle cares
   Through gazing on the unquiet sky.
And when an hour with calmer wings
Its down upon my spirit flings—
   That little time with lyre and rhyme
To while away—forbidden things !
   My heart would feel to be a crime,
Unless it trembled with the strings.

ALONE

From childhood's hour I have not been
As others were,—I have not seen
As others saw,—I could not bring
My passions from a common spring.
From the same source I have not taken
My sorrow; I could not awaken

*Edgar
Allan
Poe*

My heart to joy at the same tone;
And all I loved, *I* loved alone.
Then—in my childhood—in the dawn
Of a most stormy life was drawn
From every depth of good and ill
The mystery which binds me still:
From the torrent, or the fountain,
From the red cliff of the mountain,
From the sun that round me rolled
In its autumn tint of gold,—
From the lightning in the sky
As it passed me flying by,—
From the thunder and the storm,
And the cloud that took the form
(When the rest of Heaven was blue)
Of a demon in my view.

*John
Clare*

THE THRUSH'S NEST

Within a thick and spreading hawthorn bush,
That overhung a molehill large and round,
I heard from morn to morn a merry thrush
Sing hymns to sunrise, and I drank the sound
With joy; and, often an intruding guest,
I watched her secret toils from day to day,—
How true she warped the moss to form a nest,
And modelled it within with wood and clay;
And by and by, like heath-bells gilt with dew,
There lay her shining eggs, as bright as flowers,
Ink-spotted-over, shells of greeny blue;
And there I witnessed, in the sunny hours,
A brood of Nature's minstrels chirp and fly,
Glad as that sunshine and the laughing sky.

FIRST SIGHT OF SPRING

John
Clare

The hazel-blooms, in threads of crimson hue,
Peep through the swelling buds, foretelling
 Spring,
Ere yet a white-thorn leaf appears in view,
Or March finds throstles pleased enough to sing.
To the old touchwood tree woodpeckers cling
A moment, and their harsh-toned notes renew;
In happier mood, the stockdove claps his wing;
The squirrel sputters up the powdered oak,
With tail cocked o'er his head, and ears erect,
Startled to hear the woodman's understroke;
And with the courage which his fears collect,
He hisses fierce half malice and half glee,
Leaping from branch to branch about the tree,
In winter's foliage, moss and lichens, deckt.

From WHAT IS LIFE?

And what is Life?—An hour-glass on the run,
A mist retreating from the morning sun,
A busy, bustling, still repeated dream;
Its length?—A minute's pause, a moment's
 thought;
And happiness?—A bubble on the stream,
That in the act of seizing shrinks to nought.

What are vain Hopes?—The puffing gale of
 morn,
That of its charms divests the dewy lawn,

John
Clare And robs each flow'ret of its gem,—and dies;
A cobweb hiding disappointment's thorn,
Which stings more keenly through the thin disguise.

I AM !

(Written in Northampton County Asylum)

I am ! yet what I am who cares, or knows ?
    My friends forsake me, like a memory lost.
I am the self-consumer of my woes;
    They rise and vanish, an oblivious host,
Shadows of life, whose very soul is lost.
And yet I am—I live—though I am tossed.

Into the nothingness of scorn and noise,
    Into the living sea of waking dream,
Where there is neither sense of life, nor joys,
    But the huge shipwreck of my own esteem
And all that's dear.   Even those I loved the best
Are strange—nay, they are stranger than the rest.

I long for scenes where man has never trod—
    For scenes where woman never smiled or wept—
There to abide with my Creator, God,
    And sleep as I in childhood sweetly slept,
Full of high thoughts, unborn.   So let me lie,—
The grass below; above, the vaulted sky.

REMEMBRANCE

*Emily
Brontë*

Cold in the earth—and the deep snow piled
    above thee,
Far, far removed, cold in the dreary grave !
Have I forgot, my only Love, to love thee,
Severed at last by Time's all-severing wave ?

Now, when alone, do my thoughts no longer
    hover
Over the mountains, on that northern shore,
Resting their wings where heath and fern-
    leaves cover
Thy noble heart for ever, ever more ?

Cold in the earth—and fifteen wild Decembers
From those brown hills have melted into spring :
Faithful, indeed, is the spirit that remembers
After such years of change and suffering !

Sweet Love of youth, forgive, if I forget thee,
While the world's tide is bearing me along ;
Other desires and other hopes beset me,
Hopes which obscure, but cannot do thee
    wrong !

No later light has lightened up my heaven,
No second morn has ever shone for me ;
All my life's bliss from thy dear life was given,
All my life's bliss is in the grave with thee.

But, when the days of golden dreams had
    perished,
And even Despair was powerless to destroy ;
Then did I learn how existence could be cherished,
Strengthened, and fed without the aid of joy.

Emily Then did I check the tears of useless passion—
Brontë Weaned my young soul from yearning after
thine;
Sternly denied its burning wish to hasten
Down to that tomb already more than mine.

And, even yet, I dare not let it languish,
Dare not indulge in memory's rapturous pain;
Once drinking deep of that divinest anguish,
How could I seek the empty world again?

From A POEM BEGINNING " HOW
CLEAR SHE SHINES ! "

I'll think, there's not one world above,
　　Far as these straining eyes can see,
Where Wisdom ever laughed at Love,
　　Or Virtue crouched to Infamy;
Where, writhing 'neath the stroke of Fate,
　　The mangled wretch was forced to smile,
To match his patience 'gainst her hate,
　　His heart rebellious all the while;
Where Pleasure still will lead to wrong,
　　And helpless Reason warn in vain;
And Truth is weak, and Treachery strong;
　　And Joy the surest path to Pain;
And Peace, the lethargy of Grief;
　　And Hope, a phantom of the soul;
And Life, a labour, void and brief;
　　And Death, the despot of the whole !

"I THOUGHT ONCE . . ."

Elizabeth Barrett Browning

I thought once how Theocritus had sung
  Of the sweet years, the dear and wished for
    years,
  Who each one in a gracious hand appears
To bear a gift for mortals old or young:
And, as I mused it in his antique tongue,
  I saw, in gradual vision through my tears,
  The sweet, sad years, the melancholy years—
Those of my own life, who by turns had flung
A shadow across me.   Straightway I was 'ware,
  So weeping, how a mystic Shape did move
Behind me, and drew me backward by the hair;
  And a voice said in mastery, while I strove,
" Guess now who holds thee ? "—" Death," I
    said.   But, there,
  The silver answer rang—" Not Death, but
    Love."

"UNLIKE ARE WE . . ."

Unlike are we, unlike, O princely Heart !
  Unlike our uses, and our destinies.
  Our ministering two angels look surprise
On one another, as they strike athwart
Their wings in passing.   Thou, bethink thee,
    art
  A guest for queens to social pageantries,
  With gages from a hundred brighter eyes

Than tears even can make mine, to ply thy
part
Of chief musician.   What hast *thou* to do
    With looking from the lattice-lights at me,
A poor, tired, wandering singer ?—singing
    through
    The dark, and leaning up a cypress tree ?
Thechrism is on thine head,—on mine the dew,—
    And Death must dig the level where these
    agree.

"IF THOU MUST LOVE ME . . ."

If thou must love me, let it be for nought
    Except for love's sake only.   Do not say,
    " I love her for her smile—her look—her way
Of speaking gently—for a trick of thought
That falls in well with mine, and certes brought
    A sense of pleasant ease on such a day "—
    For these things in themselves, Beloved, may
Be changed, or change for thee,—and love, so
    wrought,
May be unwrought so.   Neither love me for
    Thine own dear pity's wiping my cheeks dry,—
A creature might forget to weep, who bore
    Thy comfort long, and lose thy love thereby !
But love me for love's sake, that evermore
    Thou may'st love on, through love's eternity.

CUI BONO?

*Thomas
Carlyle*

What is Hope ?   A smiling rainbow
 Children follow through the wet;
'Tis not here, still yonder, yonder:
 Never urchin found it yet.

What is Life ?   A thawing iceboard
 On a sea with sunny shore;—
Gay we sail; it melts beneath us;
 We are sunk, and seen no more.

What is Man ?   A foolish baby,
 Vainly strives, and fights, and frets;
Demanding all, deserving nothing;—
 One small grave is what he gets.

"WHERE LIES THE LAND . . ."

*Arthur
Hugh
Clough*

Where lies the land to which the ship would go?
Far, far ahead, is all her seamen know.
And where the land she travels from ?   Away,
Far, far behind, is all that they can say.

On sunny noons upon the deck's smooth face,
Linked arm in arm, how pleasant here to pace;
Or, o'er the stern reclining, watch below
The foaming wake far widening as we go;

Arthur
Hugh
Clough
On stormy nights when wild north-westers rave,
How proud a thing to fight with wind and wave!
The dripping sailor on the reeling mast
Exults to bear, and scorns to wish it past.

Where lies the land to which the ship would go?
Far, far ahead, is all her seamen know.
And where the land she travels from?   Away,
Far, far behind, is all that they can say.

THE LATEST DECALOGUE

Thou shalt have one God only; who
Would be at the expense of two?
No graven images may be
Worshipped, except the currency.
Swear not at all; for, for thy curse
Thine enemy is none the worse.
At church on Sunday to attend
Will serve to keep the world thy friend.
Honour thy parents; that is, all
From whom advancement may befall.
Thou shalt not kill; but need'st not strive
Officiously to keep alive.
Do not adultery commit;
Advantage rarely comes of it.
Thou shalt not steal; an empty feat,
When it's so lucrative to cheat.
Bear not false witness; let the lie
Have time on its own wings to fly.
Thou shalt not covet, but tradition
Approves all forms of competition.

44

GIVE ALL TO LOVE

Ralph Waldo Emerson

Give all to love;
Obey thy heart;
Friends, kindred, days,
Estate, good-fame,
Plans, credit, and the Muse,—
Nothing refuse.

'Tis a brave master;
Let it have scope:
Follow it utterly,
Hope beyond hope:
High and more high
It dives into noon,
With wing unspent,
Untold intent;
But it is a god,
Knows its own path,
And the outlets of the sky.

It was not for the mean;
It requireth courage stout,
Souls above doubt,
Valour unbending;
Such 'twill reward;—
They shall return
More than they were,
And ever ascending.

Leave all for love;
Yet, hear me, yet,
One word more thy heart behoved,

One pulse more of firm endeavour,—
Keep thee to-day,
To-morrow, forever,
Free as an Arab
Of thy beloved.

Cling with life to the maid;
But when the surprise,
First vague shadow of surmise,
Flits across her bosom young
Of a joy apart from thee,
Free be she, fancy-free;
Nor thou detain her vesture's hem,
Nor the palest rose she flung
From her summer diadem.

Though thou loved her as thyself,
As a self of purer clay;
Though her parting dims the day,
Stealing grace from all alive;
Heartily know,
When half-gods go
The gods arrive.

TO THE HUMBLE-BEE

Burly, dozing humble-bee,
Where thou art is clime for me.
Let them sail for Porto Rique,
Far-off heats through seas to seek;
I will follow thee alone,
Thou animated torrid-zone!

Zigzag steerer, desert cheerer,
Let me chase thy waving lines;
Keep me nearer, me thy hearer,
Singing over shrubs and vines.

Ralph
Waldo
Emerson

Insect lover of the sun,
Joy of thy dominion !
Sailor of the atmosphere;
Swimmer through the waves of air;
Voyager of light and noon;
Epicurean of June;
Wait, I prithee, till I come
Within earshot of thy hum,—
All without is martyrdom.

When the south wind, in May days,
With a net of shining haze
Silvers the horizon wall,
And, with softness touching all,
Tints the human countenance
With a colour of romance,
And, infusing subtle heats,
Turns the sod to violets,
Thou, in sunny solitudes,
Rover of the underwoods,
The green silence dost displace
With thy mellow, breezy bass.

Hot midsummer's petted crone !
Sweet to me thy drowsy tone
Tells of countless sunny hours,
Long days, and solid banks of flowers;

Of gulfs of sweetness without bound
In Indian wildernesses found;
Of Syrian peace, immortal leisure,
Firmest cheer, and bird-like pleasure.

Aught unsavoury or unclean
Hath my insect never seen;
But violets and bilberry bells,
Maple-sap, and daffodels,
Grass with green flag half-mast high,
Succory to match the sky,
Columbine with horn of honey,
Scented fern, and agrimony,
Clover, catchfly, adder's-tongue,
And brier-roses dwelt among;
All beside was unknown waste,
All was picture as he passed.

Wiser far than human seer,
Yellow-breeched philosopher !
Seeing only what is fair,
Sipping only what is sweet,
Thou dost mock at fate and care,
Leave the chaff, and take the wheat.
When the fierce northwestern blast
Cools sea and land so far and fast,
Thou already slumberest deep;
Woe and want thou canst outsleep;
Want and woe, which torture us,
Thy sleep makes ridiculous.

TOKENS

William Barnes

Green mwold on zummer bars do show
That they've a-dripp'd in winter wet;
The hoof-worn ring o' groun' below
The tree, do tell o' storms or het;
The trees in rank along a ledge
Do show where woonce did bloom a hedge;
An' where the vurrow-marks do stripe
The down, the wheat woonce rustled ripe.
Each mark ov things a-gone vrom view—
To eyezight's woone, to soulzight two.

The grass ageän the mwoldrèn door
'S a token sad o' vo'k a-gone,
An' where the house, bwoth wall an' vloor,
'S a-lost, the well mid linger on.
What tokens, then, could Meäry gi'e
Thät she'd a-liv'd, an' liv'd vor me,
But things a-done vor thought an' view?
Good things that nwone ageän can do,
An' every work her love ha' wrought,
To eyezight's woone, but two to thought.

TO THE DRIVING CLOUD

Henry Wadsworth Longfellow

Gloomy and dark art thou, O chief of the mighty
    Omahas;
Gloomy and dark, as the driving cloud, whose
    name thou hast taken!
Wrapt in thy scarlet blanket, I see thee stalk
    through the city's

Narrow and populous streets, as once by the
    margin of rivers
Stalked those birds unknown, that have left us
    only their footprints.
What, in a few short years, will remain of thy
    race but the footprints ?

How canst thou walk these streets, who hast
    trod the green turf of the prairies ?
How canst thou breathe this air, who
    hast breathed the sweet air of the
    mountains ?
Ah ! 'tis vain that with lordly looks of disdain
    thou dost challenge
Looks of disdain in return, and question these
    walls and these pavements,
Claiming the soil for thy hunting-grounds, while
    down-trodden millions
Starve in the garrets of Europe, and cry from its
    caverns that they, too,
Have been created heirs of the earth, and claim
    its division !

Back, then, back to thy woods in the regions
    west of the Wabash !
There as a monarch thou reignest.   In autumn
    the leaves of the maple
Pave the floors of thy palace-halls with gold, and
    in summer
Pine-trees waft through its chambers the odorous
    breath of their branches.
There thou art strong and great, a hero, a tamer
    of horses !

50

There thou chasest the stately stag on the banks *Henry*
   of the Elk-horn, *Wadsworth*
Or by the roar of the Running-Water, or where *Longfellow*
   the Omaha
Calls thee, and leaps through the wild ravine
   like a brave of the Blackfeet !

Hark ! what murmurs arise from the heart of
   those mountainous deserts ?
Is it the cry of the Foxes and Crows, or the
   mighty Behemoth,
Who, unharmed, on his tusks once caught the
   bolts of the thunder,
And now lurks in his lair to destroy the race of
   the red man ?
Far more fatal to thee and thy race than the
   Crows and the Foxes,
Far more fatal to thee and thy race than the
   tread of Behemoth,
Lo ! the big thunder-canoe, that steadily breasts
   the Missouri's
Merciless current ! and yonder, afar on the
   prairies, the camp-fires
Gleam through the night ; and the cloud of dust
   in the grey of the daybreak
Marks not the buffalo's track, nor the Mandan's
   dexterous horse-race ;
It is a caravan, whitening the desert where dwell
   the Comanches !
Ha ! how the breath of these Saxons and Celts,
   like the blast of the east-wind,
Drifts evermore to the west the scanty smokes
   of thy wigwams !

THE JEWISH CEMETERY AT NEWPORT

How strange it seems !   These Hebrews in their
    graves,
  Close by the street of this fair seaport town,
Silent beside the never-silent waves,
  At rest in all this moving up and down.

The trees are white with dust, that o'er their
    sleep
  Wave their broad curtains in the south wind's
    breath,
While underneath such leafy tents they keep
  The long mysterious Exodus of Death.

And these sepulchral stones, so old and brown,
  That pave with level flags their burial-place,
Seem like the tablets of the Law, thrown down
  And broken by Moses at the mountain's base.

The very names recorded here are strange,
  Of foreign accent, and of different climes;
Alvares and Rivera interchange
  With Abraham and Jacob of old times.

" Blessed be God ! for he created Death ! "
  The mourner said, " and Death is rest and
    peace ; "
Then added, in the certainty of faith,
  " And giveth Life that never more shall
    cease."

Closed are the portals of their Synagogue,
  No Psalms of David now the silence break,
No Rabbi reads the ancient Decalogue
  In the grand dialect the Prophets spake.

*Henry
Wadsworth
Longfellow*

Gone are the living, but the dead remain,
  And not neglected; for a hand unseen,
Scattering its bounty, like a summer rain,
  Still keeps their graves and their remembrance
    green.

How came they here?   What burst of Christian
    hate,
  What persecution, merciless and blind,
Drove o'er the sea—that desert desolate—
  These Ishmaels and Hagars of mankind?

They lived in narrow streets and lanes obscure,
  Ghetto and Judenstrass, in mirk and mire;
Taught in the school of patience to endure
  The life of anguish and the death of fire.

All their lives long, with the unleavened bread
  And bitter herbs of exile and its fears,
The wasting famine of the heart they fed,
  And slaked its thirst with Marah of their tears.

Anathema maranatha! was the cry
  That rang from town to town, from street to
    street;
At every gate the accursed Mordecai
  Was mocked and jeered, and spurned by
    Christian feet.

Henry
Wadsworth
Longfellow
Pride and humiliation hand in hand
  Walked with them through the world where'er
    they went;
Trampled and beaten were they as the sand,
  And yet unshaken as the continent.

For in the background figures vague and vast
  Of patriarchs and of prophets rose sublime,
And all the great traditions of the Past
  They saw reflected in the coming time.

And thus for ever with reverted look
  The mystic volume of the world they read,
Spelling it backward, like a Hebrew book,
  Till life became a Legend of the Dead.

But ah ! what once has been shall be no more !
  The groaning earth in travail and in pain
Brings forth its races, but does not restore,
  And the dead nations never rise again.

Edward
Fitzgerald
QUATRAINS From THE RUBÁIYÁT
OF OMAR KHAYYÁM

Awake ! for Morning in the bowl of Night
Has flung the stone that puts the stars to flight :
  And lo ! the Hunter of the East has caught
The Sultán's turret in a noose of light.

Come, fill the cup, and in the fire of Spring
The winter garment of repentance fling :
  The Bird of Time has but a little way
To fly—and lo ! the Bird is on the wing.

Look to the Rose that blows about us—" Lo, *Edward*
Laughing," she says, " into the world I blow: *Fitzgerald*
   At once the silken tassel of my purse
Tear, and its treasure on the garden throw."

The worldly hope men set their hearts upon
Turns ashes—or it prospers; and anon,
   Like snow upon the desert's dusty face
Lighting a little hour or two—is gone.

And those who husbanded the golden grain,
And those who flung it to the winds like rain,
   Alike to no such aureate earth are turned
As, buried once, men want dug up again.

They say the lion and the lizard keep
The courts where Jamshýd gloried and drank
     deep;
   And Bahram, that great hunter—the wild ass
Stamps o'er his head, and cannot break his sleep.

Think, in this battered caravanserai
Whose doorways are alternate Night and Day,
   How Sultán after Sultán with his pomp
Abode his destined hour and went his way.

One moment in annihilation's waste,
One moment of the well of life to taste—
   The stars are setting and the caravan
Starts for the dawn of nothing—oh, make
     haste !

Edward Fitzgerald Ah, my beloved, fill the cup that clears
To-day of past regrets and future fears—
    To-morrow?—Why, to-morrow I may be
Myself with yesterday's sev'n thousand years.

The moving finger writes; and, having writ,
Moves on: nor all thy piety nor wit
    Shall lure it back to cancel half a line,
Nor all thy tears wash out a word of it.

Indeed the idols I have loved so long
Have done my credit in men's eyes much wrong:
    Have drowned my honour in a shallow cup
And sold my reputation for a song.

And much as wine has played the infidel,
And robbed me of my robe of honour—well,
    I often wonder what the vintners buy
One half so precious as the goods they sell.

Ah, Moon of my Delight who know'st no wane,
The moon of Heav'n is rising once again:
    How oft hereafter rising shall she look
Through this same garden after me—in vain!

And when thyself with shining foot shall pass
Among the guests star-scattered on the grass,
    And in thy joyous errand reach the spot
Where I made one—turn down an empty glass!

A CHANTED CALENDAR
From BALDER

*Sydney
Dobell*

First came the primrose.
On the bank high,
Like a maiden looking forth
From the window of a tower
When the battle rolls below,
So looked she,
And saw the storms go by.

Then came the wind-flower
In the valley left behind,
As a wounded maiden pale
With purple streaks of woe
When the battle has rolled by
Wanders to and fro,
So tottered she,
Dishevelled in the wind.

Then came the daisies,
On the first of May,
Like a bannered show's advance
While the crowd runs by the way,
With ten thousand flowers about them they came
    trooping through the fields.
As a happy people come,
So came they,
As a happy people come
When the war has rolled away,
With dance and tabor, pipe and drum,
And all make holiday.

Sydney
Dobell

Then came the cowslip,
Like a dancer in the fair,
She spread her little mat of green,
And on it danced she.
With a fillet bound about her brow,
A fillet round her happy brow,
A golden fillet round her brow,
And rubies in her hair.

From AN AUTUMN MOOD

Pile the pyre, light the fire—there is fuel enough
    and to spare;
You have fire enough and to spare with your
    madness and gladness;
Burn the old year—it is dead, and dead, and
    done.
There is something under the sun that I cannot
    bear:
I cannot bear this sadness under the sun,
I cannot bear this sun upon all this sadness.
Here on this prophecy, here on this leafless
    log,
Log upon log, and leafless on leafless, I sit.
Yes, Beauty, I see thee; yes, I see, but I will not
    rejoice.
Down, down, wild heart! down, down, thou
    hungry dog
That dost but leap and gaze with a want thou
    canst not utter!
Down, down!   I know the ill, but where is the
    cure?

Moor and stubble and mist, stubble and mist *Sydney*
    and moor,   *Dobell*
Here, on the turf that will feel the snows, a
    vanishing flutter
Of bells that are ringing farewells,
And overhead, from a branch that will soon be
    bare,
Is it a falling leaf that disturbs my blood like a
    voice ?
Or is it an autumn bird that answers the evening
    light ?
The evening light on stubble and moor and
    mist,
And pallid woods, and the pale sweet hamlets
    of dying men.
Oh, autumn bird !   I also will speak as I
    list.
Oh, woods ! oh, fields ! oh, trees ! oh, hill and
    glen !
You who have seen my glory, you who wist
How I have walked the mornings of delight—
Myself a morning, summer'd through and
    lit
With light and summer as the sunny dew
With sun : you saw me then—
You see me now ; oh, hear my heart and answer
    it.
Where is the Nevermore and the Land of
    Yesterdays ?
      Aye,
Where are Youth and Joy, the dew and the
    honey-dew,
The day of the rose, and the night of the nightin-
    gale ?

Sydney   Where—
Dobell   Where are the sights and the sounds that shall
        ne'er and shall e'er
Come again ?
Once more I have cried my cry, once more in
        vain
I have listened; once more, for a moment, the
        ancient pain
Is less, though I know that the year is dead and
        done.
Once more I bear
Under the sun the sadness, over the sadness the
        sun.

DESOLATE

From the sad eaves the drip-drop of the rain !
The water washing at the latchel door;
A slow step plashing by upon the moor;
A single bleat far from the famished fold;
The clicking of an embered hearth and cold;
The rainy Robin tic-tac at the pane.

" So as it is with thee
Is it with me,
So as it is and it used not to be,
With thee used not to be,
Nor me."
So singeth Robin on the willow tree,
The rainy Robin tic-tac at the pane.

Here in this breast all day
The fire is dim and low,
Within I care not to stay,
Without I care not to go.

A sadness ever sings
Of unforgotten things,
And the bird of love is patting at the pane;
But the wintry water deepens at the door,
And a step is plashing by upon the moor
Into the dark upon the darkening moor,
And alas, alas, the drip-drop of the rain !

Sydney Dobell

MY EPITAPH

David Gray

Below lies one whose name was traced in sand.
He died, not knowing what it was to live:
Died, while the first sweet consciousness of man-
    hood
And maiden thought electrified his soul,
Faint beatings in the calyx of the rose.
Bewildered reader ! pass without a sigh,
In a proud sorrow !   There is life with God,
In other kingdom of a sweeter air.
In Eden every flower is blown :   Amen.

THE WITCH'S BALLAD

William Bell Scott

O I hae come from far away,
    From a warm land far away,
A southern land across the sea,
With sailor-lads about the mast,
Merry and canny, and kind to me.

61

William
Bell
Scott

And I hae been to yon town
    To try my luck in yon town;
Nort, and Mysie, Elspie too.
Right braw we were to pass the gate,
Wi' gowden clasps on girdles blue.

Mysie smiled wi' miminy mouth,
    Innocent mouth, miminy mouth;
Elspie wore a scarlet gown,
Nort's grey eyes were unco' gleg.
My Castile comb was like a crown.

We walked abreast all up the street,
    Into the market up the street;
Our hair with marigolds was wound,
Our bodices with love-knots laced,
Our merchandise with tansy bound.

Nort had chickens, I had cocks,
    Gamesome cocks, loud-crowing cocks;
Mysie ducks, and Elspie drakes,—
For a wee groat or a pound;
We lost nae time wi' gives and takes.

—Lost nae time, for well we knew,
    In our sleeves full well we knew,
When the gloaming came that night,
Duck nor drake, nor hen nor cock
Would be found by candle-light.

And when our chaffering all was done,   *William*
   All was paid for, sold and done,   *Bell*
We drew a glove on ilka hand,   *Scott*
We sweetly curtsied, each to each,
And deftly danced a saraband.

The market-lassies looked and laughed,
   Left their gear, and looked and laughed;
They made as they would join the game,
But soon their mithers, wild and wud,
With whack and screech they stopped the same.

Sae loud the tongues o' randies grew,
   The flytin' and the skirlin' grew,
At all the windows in the place,
Wi' spoons or knives, wi' needle or awl,
Was thrust out every hand and face.

And down each stair they thronged anon,
   Gentle, semple, thronged anon:
Souter and tailor, frowsy Nan,
The ancient widow young again,
Simpering behind her fan.

Without a choice, against their will,
   Doited, dazed, against their will,
The market lassie and her mither,
The farmer and his husbandman,
Hand in hand dance a' thegither.

Slow at first, but faster soon,
   Still increasing, wild and fast,
Hoods and mantles, hats and hose,
Blindly doffed and cast away,
Left them naked, heads and toes.

*William
Bell
Scott* They would have torn us limb from limb,
   Dainty limb from dainty limb;
But never one of them could win
Across the line that I had drawn
With bleeding thumb a-widdershin.

But there was Jeff the provost's son,
   Jeff the provost's only son;
There was Father Auld himsel',
The Lombard frae the hostelry,
And the lawyer Peter Fell.

All goodly men we singled out,
   Waled them well, and singled out,
And drew them by the left hand in;
Mysie the priest, and Elspie won
The Lombard, Nort the lawyer carle,
I mysel' the provost's son.

Then, with cantrip kisses seven,
   Three times round with kisses seven,
Warped and woven there spun we
Arms and legs and flaming hair,
Like a whirlwind on the sea.

Like a wind that sucks the sea,
   Over and in and on the sea,
Good sooth it was a mad delight;
And every man of all the four
Shut his eyes and laughed outright.

Laughed as long as they had breath,
   Laughed while they had sense or breath;

And close about us coiled a mist
Of gnats and midges, wasps and flies,
Like the whirlwind shaft it rist.

*William
Bell
Scott*

Drawn up I was right off my feet,
   Into the mist and off my feet;
And, dancing on each chimney-top,
I saw a thousand darling imps
Keeping time with skip and hop.

And on the provost's brave ridge-tile,
   On the provost's grand ridge-tile,
The Blackamoor first to master me
I saw, I saw that winsome smile,
The mouth that did my heart beguile,
And spoke the great Word over me,
In the land beyond the sea.

I called his name, I called aloud,
   Alas! I called on him aloud;
And then he filled his hand with stour,
And threw it towards me in the air;
My mouse flew out, I lost my power!

My lusty strength, my power were gone;
   Power was gone, and all was gone.
He will not let me love him more!
Of bell and whip and horse's tail
He cares not if I find a store.

But I am proud if he is fierce!
   I am as proud as he is fierce;
I'll turn about and backward go,
If I meet again that Blackamoor,
And he'll help us then, for he shall know
I seek another paramour.

William
Bell
Scott
And we'll gang once more to yon town,
　　Wi' better luck to yon town;
We'll walk in silk and cramoisie,
And I shall wed the provost's son
My lady of the town I'll be !

For I was born a crowned king's child,
　　Born and nursed a king's child,
King o' a land ayont the sea,
Where the Blackamoor kissed me first,
And taught me art and glamourie.

Each one in her wame shall hide
　　Her hairy mouse, her wary mouse,
Fed on madwort and agramie,—
Wear amber beads between her breasts,
And blind-worm's skin about her knee.

The Lombard shall be Elspie's man,
　　Elspie's gowden husband-man;
Nort shall take the lawyer's hand;
The priest shall swear another vow:
We'll dance again the saraband !

CHORIC SONG
From THE LOTOS-EATERS

Lord
Tennyson

There is sweet music here that softer falls
Than petals from blown roses on the grass,
Or night-dews on still waters between walls
Of shadowy granite, in a gleaming pass;
Music that gentlier on the spirit lies,
Than tired eyelids upon tired eyes;

Music that brings sweet sleep down from the *Lord*
    blissful skies.   *Tennyson*
Here are cool mosses deep,
And thro' the moss the ivies creep,
And in the stream the long-leaved flowers weep,
And from the craggy ledge the poppy hangs in
    sleep.

Why are we weighed upon with heaviness,
And utterly consumed with sharp distress,
While all things else have rest from weariness?
All things have rest: why should we toil alone,
We only toil, who are the first of things,
And make perpetual moan,
Still from one sorrow to another thrown:
Nor ever fold our wings,
And cease from wanderings,
Nor steep our brows in slumber's holy balm;
Nor harken what the inner spirit sings,
" There is no joy but calm ! "—
Why should we only toil, the roof and crown of
    things ?

Lo ! in the middle of the wood,
The folded leaf is wooed from out the bud
With winds upon the branch, and there
Grows green and broad, and takes no care,
Sun-steeped at noon, and in the moon
Nightly dew-fed; and turning yellow
Falls, and floats adown the air.
Lo ! sweetened with the summer light,
The full-juiced apple, waxing over-mellow,
Drops in a silent autumn night.
All its allotted length of days,

Lord
Tennyson
The flower ripens in its place,
Ripens and fades, and falls, and hath no toil,
Fast-rooted in the fruitful soil.

Hateful is the dark-blue sky,
Vaulted o'er the dark-blue sea.
Death is the end of life; ah, why
Should life all labour be?
Let us alone.   Time driveth onward fast,
And in a little while our lips are dumb.
Let us alone.   What is it that will last?
All things are taken from us, and become
Portions and parcels of the dreadful Past.
Let us alone.   What pleasure can we have
To war with evil?   Is there any peace
In ever climbing up the climbing wave?
All things have rest, and ripen toward the
     grave
In silence; ripen, fall and cease:
Give us long rest or death, dark death, or dream-
     ful ease.

How sweet it were, hearing the downward stream
With half-shut eyes ever to seem
Falling asleep in a half-dream!
To dream and dream, like yonder amber light,
Which will not leave the myrrh-bush on the
     height;
To hear each other's whispered speech;
Eating the Lotos day by day,
To watch the crisping ripples on the beach,
And tender curving lines of creamy spray;
To lend our hearts and spirits wholly
To the influence of mild-minded melancholy;

68

To muse and brood and live again in memory,   *Lord*
With those old faces of our infancy   *Tennyson*
Heaped over with a mound of grass,
Two handfuls of white dust, shut in an urn of
    brass !

Dear is the memory of our wedded lives,
And dear the last embraces of our wives
And their warm tears: but all hath suffered
    change;
For surely now our household hearths are cold:
Our sons inherit us: our looks are strange:
And we should come like ghosts to trouble joy.
Or else the island princes over-bold
Have eat our substance, and the minstrel sings
Before them of the ten years' war in Troy,
And our great deeds, as half-forgotten things.
Is there confusion in the little isle ?
Let what is broken so remain.
The Gods are hard to reconcile:
'Tis hard to settle order once again.

There *is* confusion worse than death,
Trouble on trouble, pain on pain,
Long labour unto aged breath,
Sore task to hearts worn out with many wars
And eyes grown dim with gazing on the pilot-
    stars.
But, propt on beds of amaranth and moly,
How sweet (while warm airs lull us, blowing
    lowly)
With half-dropt eyelid still,
Beneath a heaven dark and holy,
To watch the long bright river drawing slowly

His waters from the purple hill—
To hear the dewy echoes calling
From cave to cave through the thick-twined vine—
To watch the emerald-coloured water falling
Through many a woven acanthus-wreath divine !
Only to hear and see the far-off sparkling brine,
Only to hear were sweet, stretched out beneath
the pine.

The Lotos blooms below the barren peak :
The Lotos blows by every winding creek :
All day the wind breathes low with mellower
tone :
Through every hollow cave and alley lone
Round and round the spicy downs the yellow
Lotos-dust is blown.
We have had enough of action, and of motion we,
Rolled to starboard, rolled to larboard, when the
surge was seething free,
Where the wallowing monster spouted his foam-
fountains in the sea.

Let us swear an oath, and keep it with an equal
mind,
In the hollow Lotos-land to live and lie reclined
On the hills like Gods together, careless of mankind.
For they lie beside their nectar, and the bolts are
hurled
Far below them in the valleys, and the clouds are
lightly curled
Round their golden houses, girdled with the
gleaming world :

Where they smile in secret, looking over wasted *Lord*
    lands,   *Tennyson*
Blight and famine, plague and earthquake, roar-
    ing deeps and fiery sands,
Clanging fights, and flaming towns, and sinking
    ships, and praying hands.
But they smile, they find a music centred in a
    doleful song
Steaming up, a lamentation and an ancient tale
    of wrong,
Like a tale of little meaning though the words
    are strong;
Chanted from an ill-used race of men that cleave
    the soil,
Sow the seed, and reap the harvest with enduring
    toil,
Storing yearly little dues of wheat, and wine and
    oil;
Till they perish and they suffer—some, 'tis
    whispered—down in hell
Suffer endless anguish, others in Elysian valleys
    dwell,
Resting weary limbs at last on beds of asphodel.
Surely, surely, slumber is more sweet than toil,
    the shore
Than labour in the deep mid-ocean, wind and
    wave and oar;
O rest ye, brother mariners, we will not wander
    more.

Lord
Tennyson

Oh yet we trust that somehow good
    Will be the final goal of ill,
    To pangs of nature, sins of will,
Defects of doubt, and taints of blood;

That nothing walks with aimless feet;
    That not one life shall be destroyed,
    Or cast as rubbish to the void,
When God hath made the pile complete;

That not a worm is cloven in vain;
    That not a moth with vain desire
    Is shrivelled in a fruitless fire,
Or but subserves another's gain.

Behold, we know not anything;
    I can but trust that good shall fall
    At last—far off—at last, to all,
And every winter change to spring.

So runs my dream: but what am I?
    An infant crying in the night:
    An infant crying for the light:
And with no language but a cry.

The wish, that of the living whole
    No life may fail beyond the grave,
    Derives it not from what we have,
The likest God within the soul?

Are God and Nature then at strife,
    That Nature lends such evil dreams?
    So careful of the type she seems,
So careless of the single life;

That I, considering everywhere
   Her secret meaning in her deeds,
   And finding that of fifty seeds
She often brings but one to bear,

I falter where I firmly trod,
   And falling with my weight of cares
   Upon the great world's altar-stairs
That slope through darkness up to God,

I stretch lame hands of faith, and grope,
   And gather dust and chaff, and call
   To what I feel is Lord of all,
And faintly trust the larger hope.

" So careful of the type ? " but no.
   From scarped cliff and quarried stone
   She cries, " A thousand types are gone:
I care for nothing, all shall go.

" Thou makest thine appeal to me:
   I bring to life, I bring to death:
   The spirit does but mean the breath:
I know no more."   And he, shall he,

Man, her last work, who seemed so fair,
   Such splendid purpose in his eyes,
   Who rolled the psalm to wintry skies,
Who built him fanes of fruitless prayer,

Who trusted God was love indeed
   And love Creation's final law—
   Though Nature, red in tooth and claw
With ravin, shrieked against his creed—

*Lord
Tennyson*

Who loved, who suffered countless ills,
    Who battled for the True, the Just,
    Be blown about the desert dust,
Or sealed within the iron hills ?

From MAUD

What if though her eye seemed full
Of a kind intent to me,
What if that dandy-despot, he,
That jewelled mass of millinery,
That oiled and curled Assyrian Bull
Smelling of musk and of insolence,
Her brother, from whom I keep aloof,
Who wants the finer politic sense
To mask, though but in his own behoof,
With a glassy smile his brutal scorn—
What if he had told her yestermorn
How prettily for his own sweet sake
A face of tenderness might be feigned,
And a moist mirage in desert eyes,
That so, when the rotten hustings shake
In another month to his brazen lies,
A wretched vote may be gained.

For a raven ever croaks, at my side,
Keep watch and ward, keep watch and ward,
Or thou wilt prove their tool.
Yea, too, myself from myself I guard,
For often a man's own angry pride
Is cap and bells for a fool.

74

MARIANA

*Lord
Tennyson*

With blackest moss the flower-plots
   Were thickly crusted, one and all:
The rusted nails fell from the knots
   That held the pear to the gable-wall.
The broken sheds looked sad and strange:
   Unlifted was the clinking latch;
   Weeded and worn the ancient thatch
Upon the lonely moated grange.
     She only said, " My life is dreary,
       He cometh not," she said;
     She said, " I am aweary, aweary,
       I would that I were dead ! "

Her tears fell with the dews at even;
   Her tears fell ere the dews were dried;
She could not look on the sweet heaven,
   Either at morn or eventide.
After the flitting of the bats,
   When thickest dark did trance the sky,
   She drew her casement-curtain by,
And glanced athwart the glooming flats.
     She only said, " The night is dreary,
       He cometh not," she said;
     She said, " I am aweary, aweary,
       I would that I were dead ! "

Upon the middle of the night,
   Waking she heard the night-fowl crow:
The cock sung out an hour ere light:
   From the dark fen the oxen's low

Came to her: without hope of change,
　　In sleep she seemed to walk forlorn,
　　Till cold winds woke the grey-eyed morn
About the lonely moated grange.
　　　　She only said, " The day is dreary,
　　　　　　He cometh not," she said;
　　　　She said, " I am aweary, aweary,
　　　　　　I would that I were dead ! "

About a stone-cast from the wall
　　A sluice with blackened waters slept,
And o'er it many, round and small,
　　The clustered marish-mosses crept.
Hard by a poplar shook alway,
　　All silver-green with gnarled bark:
　　For leagues no other tree did mark
The level waste, the rounding grey.
　　　　She only said, " My life is dreary,
　　　　　　He cometh not," she said;
　　　　She said, " I am aweary, aweary,
　　　　　　I would that I were dead ! "

And ever when the moon was low,
　　And the shrill winds were up and away,
In the white curtain, to and fro,
　　She saw the gusty shadow sway.
But when the moon was very low,
　　And wild winds bound within their cell,
　　The shadow of the poplar fell
Upon her bed, across her brow.
　　　　She only said, " The night is dreary,
　　　　　　He cometh not," she said;
　　　　She said, " I am aweary, aweary,
　　　　　　I would that I were dead ! "

All day within the dreamy house,
    The doors upon their hinges creaked;
The blue fly sung in the pane; the mouse
    Behind the mouldering wainscot shrieked,
Or from the crevice peered about.
    Old faces glimmered through the doors,
    Old footsteps trod the upper floors,
Old voices called her from without.
        She only said, " My life is dreary,
            He cometh not," she said;
        She said, " I am aweary, aweary,
            I would that I were dead ! "

The sparrow's chirrup on the roof,
    The slow clock ticking, and the sound
Which to the wooing wind aloof
    The poplar made, did all confound
Her sense; but most she loathed the hour
    When the thick-moted sunbeam lay
    Athwart the chambers, and the day
Was sloping towards his western bower.
        Then, said she, " I am very dreary,
            He will not come," she said;
        She wept, " I am aweary, aweary,
            O God, that I were dead ! "

Lord
Tennyson

ULYSSES

It little profits that an idle king,
By this still hearth, among these barren
    crags,
Matched with an aged wife, I mete and dole
Unequal laws unto a savage race,

That hoard, and sleep, and feed, and know not
me.
I cannot rest from travel: I will drink
Life to the lees; all times I have enjoyed
Greatly, have suffered greatly, both with those
That loved me, and alone; on shore, and when
Through scudding drifts the rainy Hyades
Vext the dim sea: I am become a name;
For always roaming with a hungry heart
Much have I seen and known; cities of men
And manners, climates, councils, governments,
Myself not least, but honoured of them all;
And drunk delight of battle with my peers,
Far on the ringing plains of windy Troy.
I am a part of all that I have met;
Yet all experience is an arch wherethrough
Gleams that untravelled world, whose margin
fades
For ever and for ever when I move.
How dull it is to pause, to make an end,
To rust unburnished, not to shine in use !
As though to breathe were life. Life piled on life
Were all too little, and of one to me
Little remains; but every hour is saved
From that eternal silence, something more,
A bringer of new things; and vile it were
For some three suns to store and hoard
myself,
And this grey spirit yearning in desire
To follow knowledge like a sinking star,
Beyond the utmost bound of human thought.
This is my son, mine own Telemachus,
To whom I leave the sceptre and the isle—
Well-loved of me, discerning to fulfil

This labour, by slow prudence to make mild Lord
A rugged people, and through soft degrees Tennyson
Subdue them to the useful and the good.
Most blameless is he, centred in the sphere
Of common duties, decent not to fail
In offices of tenderness, and pay
Meet adoration to my household gods,
When I am gone. He works his work, I
    mine.

      There lies the port; the vessel puffs her
    sail:
There gloom the dark broad seas. My
    mariners,
Souls that have toiled, and wrought, and thought
    with me—
That ever with a frolic welcome took
The thunder and the sunshine, and opposed
Free hearts, free foreheads—you and I are old;
Old age hath yet his honour and his toil;
Death closes all; but something ere the end,
Some work of noble note, may yet be done,
Not unbecoming men that strove with Gods.
The lights begin to twinkle from the rocks:
The long day wanes: the slow moon climbs: the
    deep
Moans round with many voices. Come, my
    friends,
'Tis not too late to seek a newer world.
Push off, and sitting well in order smite
The sounding furrows; for my purpose holds
To sail beyond the sunset, and the baths
Of all the western stars, until I die.
It may be that the gulfs will wash us down:

Lord
Tennyson
It may be we shall touch the Happy Isles,
And see the great Achilles, whom we knew.
Though much is taken, much abides; and though
We are not now that strength which in old days
Moved earth and heaven; that which we are, we
    are;
One equal temper of heroic hearts,
Made weak by time and fate, but strong in will
To strive, to seek, to find, and not to yield.

POEM From THE PRINCESS

  Now sleeps the crimson petal, now the white;
Nor waves the cypress in the palace walk;
Nor winks the gold fin in the porphyry font:
The fire-fly wakens: waken thou with me.

  Now droops the milkwhite peacock like a
    ghost,
And like a ghost she glimmers on to me.

  Now lies the Earth all Danaë to the stars,
And all thy heart lies open unto me.

  Now slides the silent meteor on, and leaves
A shining furrow, as thy thoughts in me.

  Now folds the lily all her sweetness up,
And slips into the bosom of the lake:
So fold thyself, my dearest, thou, and slip
Into my bosom and be lost in me.

THE BISHOP ORDERS HIS TOMB AT SAINT PRAXED'S CHURCH

Robert Browning

Vanity, saith the preacher, vanity !
Draw round my bed: is Anselm keeping back ?
Nephews—sons mine . . . ah God, I know not !
    Well—
She, men would have to be your mother once,
Old Gandolf envied me, so fair she was !
What's done is done, and she is dead beside.
Dead long ago, and I am Bishop since,
And as she died so must we die ourselves,
And thence ye may perceive the world's a dream.
Life, how and what is it ?   As here I lie
In this state-chamber, dying by degrees,
Hours and long hours in the dead night, I ask
"Do I live, am I dead ?" Peace, peace seems all.
Saint Praxed's ever was the church for peace;
And so, about this tomb of mine.   I fought
With tooth and nail to save my niche, ye know:
—Old Gandolf cozened me, despite my care;
Shrewd was that snatch from out the corner
    South
He graced his carrion with, God curse the
    same !
Yet still my niche is not so cramped but thence
One sees the pulpit o' the epistle-side,
And somewhat of the choir, those silent seats,
And up into the aery dome where live
The angels, and a sunbeam's sure to lurk:
And I shall fill my slab of basalt there,
And 'neath my tabernacle take my rest,
With those nine columns round me, two and
    two,

The odd one at my feet where Anselm stands:
Peach-blossom marble all, the rare, the ripe
As fresh-poured red wine of a mighty pulse.
—Old Gandolf with his paltry onion-stone,
Put me where I may look at him ! True peach
Rosy and flawless: how I earned the prize !
Draw close: that conflagration of my church
—What then ? So much was saved if aught were
    missed !
My sons, ye would not be my death ? Go dig
The white-grape vineyard where the oil-press
    stood
Drop water gently till the surface sink,
And if ye find. . . . Ah God, I know not,
    I ! . . .
Bedded in store of rotten fig-leaves soft,
And corded up in a tight olive-frail,
Some lump, ah God, of lapis lazuli,
Big as a Jew's head cut off at the nape.
Blue as a vein o'er the Madonna's breast . . .
Sons, all have I bequeathed you, villas, all,
That brave Frascati villa with its bath,
So, let the blue lump poise between my knees,
Like God the Father's globe on both his hands
Ye worship in the Jesu Church so gay,
For Gandolf shall not choose but see and burst !
Swift as a weaver's shuttle fleet our years:
Man goeth to the grave, and where is he ?
Did I say basalt for my slab, sons ? Black—
'Twas ever antique-black I meant ! How else
Shall ye contrast my frieze to come beneath ?
The bas-relief in bronze ye promised me,
Those Pans and Nymphs ye wot of, and per-
    chance

Some tripod, thyrsus, with a vase or so,   *Robert*
The Saviour at his sermon on the mount,   *Browning*
Saint Praxed in a glory, and one Pan
Ready to twitch the Nymph's last garment off,
And Moses with the tables . . . but I know
Ye mark me not !   What do they whisper thee,
Child of my bowels, Anselm ?   Ah, ye hope
To revel down my villas while I gasp
Bricked o'er with beggar's mouldy travertine
Which Gandolf from his tomb-top chuckles at !
Nay, boys, ye love me—all of jasper, then !
'Tis jasper ye stand pledged to, lest I grieve
My bath must needs be left behind, alas !
One block, pure green as a pistachio-nut,
There's plenty jasper somewhere in the world—
And have I not Saint Praxed's ear to pray
Horses for ye, and brown Greek manuscripts,
And mistresses with great smooth marbly
        limbs ?
—That's if ye carve my epitaph aright,
Choice Latin, picked phrase, Tully's every
        word,
No gaudy ware like Gandolf's second line—
Tully, my masters ?   Ulpian serves his need !
And then how I shall lie through centuries,
And hear the blessed mutter of the mass,
And see God made and eaten all day long,
And feel the steady candle-flame, and taste
Good strong thick stupefying incense-smoke !
For as I lie here, hours of the dead night,
Dying in state and by such slow degrees,
I fold my arms as if they clasped a crook,
And stretch my feet forth straight as stone can
        point,

And let the bedclothes, for a mortcloth, drop
Into great laps and folds of sculptor's-work:
And as yon tapers dwindle, and strange
    thoughts
Grow, with a certain humming in my ears,
About the life before I lived this life,
And this life too, popes, cardinals and priests,
Saint Praxed at his sermon on the mount,
Your tall pale mother with her talking eyes,
And new-found agate urns as fresh as day,
And marble's language, Latin pure, discreet,
—Aha, *Elucescebat* quoth our friend?
No Tully, said I, Ulpian at the best!
Evil and brief hath been my pilgrimage.
All lapis, all, sons!   Else I give the Pope
My villas!   Will ye ever eat my heart?
Ever your eyes were as a lizard's quick,
They glitter like your mother's for my soul,
Or ye would heighten my impoverished frieze,
Piece out its starved design, and fill my vase
With grapes, and add a vizor and a Term,
And to the tripod ye would tie a lynx
That in his struggle throws the thyrsus down,
To comfort me on my entablature
Whereon I am to lie till I must ask
" Do I live, am I dead? " There, leave me,
    there!
For ye have stabbed me with ingratitude
To death—ye wish it—God, ye wish it! Stone—
Gritstone, a-crumble! Clammy squares which
    sweat
As if the corpse they keep were oozing through—
And no more lapis to delight the world!
Well go! I bless ye.   Fewer tapers there,

But in a row: and, going, turn your backs Robert
—Ay, like departing altar-ministrants, Browning
And leave me in my church, the church for peace,
That I may watch at leisure if he leers—
Old Gandolf, at me, from his onion-stone,
As still he envied me, so fair she was !

A TOCCATA OF GALUPPI'S

O, Galuppi, Baldassaro, this is very sad to find !
I can hardly misconceive you; it would prove
    me deaf and blind;
But although I take your meaning, 'tis with such
    a heavy mind !

Here you come with your old music, and here's
    all the good it brings.
What, they lived once thus at Venice where the
    merchants were the kings,
Where St. Mark's is, where the Doges used to
    wed the sea with rings ?

Ay, because the sea's the street there; and 'tis
    arched by . . . what you call
. . . . Shylock's bridge with houses on it, where
    they kept the carnival:
I was never out of England—it's as if I saw
    it all !

Did young people take their pleasure when the
    sea was warm in May ?
Balls and masks begun at midnight, burning
    ever to mid-day
When they made up fresh adventures for the
    morrow, do you say ?

Was a lady such a lady, cheeks so round and lips
so red,—
On her neck the small face buoyant, like a bell-
flower on its bed,
O'er the breast's superb abundance where a
man might base his head?

Well, (and it was graceful of them) they'd break
talk off and afford
—She, to bite her mask's black velvet, he, to
finger on his sword,
While you sat and play'd Toccatas, stately at
the clavichord?

What? Those lesser thirds so plaintive, sixths
diminished, sigh on sigh,
Told them something? Those suspensions,
those solutions—" Must we die? "
Those commiserating sevenths—" Life might
last! we can but try! "

" Were you happy? "—" Yes."—" And are
you still as happy? "—" Yes. And you? "
—" Then, more kisses! "—" Did *I* stop them,
when a million seemed so few? "
Hark! the dominant's persistence, till it must
be answered to!

So an octave struck the answer. O, they praised
you, I dare say!
" Brave Galuppi! that was music! good alike
at grave and gay!
I can always leave off talking, when I hear a
master play."

Then they left you for their pleasure: till in due *Robert*
    time, one by one,   *Browning*
Some with lives that came to nothing, some with
    deeds as well undone,
Death came tacitly and took them where they
    never see the sun.

But when I sit down to reason, think to take my
    stand nor swerve,
While I triumph o'er a secret wrung from nature's
    close reserve,
In you come with your cold music, till I creep
    through every nerve.

Yes, you, like a ghostly cricket, creaking where
    a house was burned—
Dust and ashes, dead and done with, Venice
    spent what Venice earned !
The soul, doubtless, is immortal—where a soul
    can be discerned.

Yours for instance, you know physics, some-
    thing of geology,
Mathematics are your pastime; souls shall rise
    in their degree;
Butterflies may dread extinction,—you'll not
    die, it cannot be !

As for Venice and its people, merely born to
    bloom and drop,
Here on earth they bore their fruitage, mirth
    and folly were the crop:
What of soul was left, I wonder, when the kissing
    had to stop ?

" Dust and ashes ! " So you creak it, and I want
the heart to scold.
Dear dead women, with such hair, too—what's
become of all the gold
Used to hang and brush their bosoms ? I feel
chilly and grown old.

SOLILOQUY OF THE SPANISH
CLOISTER

Gr-r-r—there go, my heart's abhorrence !
Water your damned flower-pots, do !
If hate killed men, Brother Lawrence,
God's blood, would not mine kill you !
What ? Your myrtle-bush wants trimming ?
Oh, that rose has prior claims—
Needs its leaden vase filled brimming ?
Hell dry you up with its flames !

At the meal we sit together:
Salve tibi! I must hear
Wise talk of the kind of weather,
Sort of season, time of year:
Not a plenteous corn-crop: scarcely
Dare we hope oak-galls, I doubt.
What's the Latin name for " parsley " ?
What's the Greek name for Swine's snout ?

Whew ! we'll have our platter burnished,
Laid with care on our own shelf !
With a fire-new spoon we've furnished,
And a goblet for ourself,

Rinsed like something sacrificial
Ere 'tis fit to touch our chaps—
Marked with L. for our initial !
(He-he !   There his lily snaps !)

Robert
Browning

Saint, forsooth !   While brown Dolores
Squats outside the Convent bank
With Sanchicha, telling stories,
Steeping tresses in the tank,
Blue-black, lustrous, thick like horsehairs,
—Can't I see his dead eye glow,
Bright as 'twere a Barbary corsair's ?
(That is, if he'd let it show !)

When he finishes refection,
Knife and fork he never lays
Cross-wise, to my recollection,
As do I, in Jesu's praise.
I the Trinity illustrate,
Drinking watered orange-pulp—
In three sips the Avian frustrate;
While he drains his at one gulp.

Oh, those melons ?   If he's able
We're to have a feast ! so nice !
One goes to the Abbot's table,
All of us get each a slice.
How go on your flowers ? none double,
Not one fruit-sort can you spy ?
Strange !—And I, too, at such trouble,
Keep them close-nipped on the sly !

89

There's a great text in Galatians,
Once you trip on it, entails
Twenty-nine distinct damnations,
One sure, if another fails:
If I trip him just a-dying,
Sure of heaven as sure can be,
Spin him round and send him flying
Off to hell, a Manichee?

Or, my scrofulous French novel
On grey paper with blunt type !
Simply glance at it, you grovel
Hand and foot in Belial's gripe.
If I double down its pages
At the woeful sixteenth print,
When he gathers his greengages
Ope a sieve and slip it in't ?

Or, there's Satan !—One might venture
Pledge one's soul to him, yet leave
Such a flaw in the indenture
As He'd miss till, past retrieve,
Blasted lay that rose-acacia
We're so proud of !   *Hy, Zy, Hine* . . .
'St, there's Vespers !   *Plena gratia*
Ave, Virgo ! Gr-r-r—you swine !

SONG From PARACELSUS

Heap cassia, sandal-buds and stripes
    Of labdanum, and aloe-balls,
Smeared with dull nard an Indian wipes
    From out her hair: (such balsam falls

90

Down sea-side mountain pedestals,   *Robert*
From tree-tops where tired winds are fain,   *Browning*
Spent with the vast and howling main,
To treasure half their island-gain.)

And strew faint sweetness from some old
    Egyptian's fine worm-eaten shroud
Which breaks to dust when once unrolled;
    Or shredded perfume, like a cloud
    From closet long to quiet vowed,
With mothed and dropping arras hung,
Mouldering the lute and books among
Of queen, long dead, who lived there young.

MISCONCEPTIONS

This is a spray the Bird clung to,
    Making it blossom with pleasure,
Ere the high tree-top she sprung to,
    Fit for her nest and her treasure.
    O, what a hope beyond measure
Was the poor spray's which the flying feet hung
        to,—
So to be singled out, built in, and sung to !

This is a heart the Queen leant on,
    Thrilled in a minute erratic,
Ere the true bosom she bent on,
    Meet for love's regal dalmatic.
    O, what a fancy ecstatic
Was the poor heart's, ere the wanderer went on—
Love to be saved for it, proffered to, spent on

IN A GONDOLA

The moth's kiss, first !
Kiss me as if you made believe
You were not sure, this eve,
How my face, your flower, had pursed
Its petals up; so, here and there
You brush it, till I grow aware
Who wants me, and wide ope I burst.

The bee's kiss, now !
Kiss me as if you entered gay
My heart at some noonday,
A bud that dares not disallow
The claim, so all is rendered up,
And passively its shattered cup
Over your head to sleep I bow.

PROSPICE

Fear death ?—to feel the fog in my throat,
    The mist in my face,
When the snows begin, and the blasts denote
    I am nearing the place,
The power of the night, the press of the storm,
    The post of the foe;
Where he stands, the Arch Fear in a visible
        form,
    Yet the strong man must go:
For the journey is done and the summit attained,
    And the barriers fall,
Though a battle's to fight ere the guerdon be
        gained,

The reward of it all.   *Robert*
I was ever a fighter, so—one fight more,   *Browning*
    The best and the last !
I would hate that death bandaged my eyes and
        forbore,
    And bade me creep past.
No ! let me taste the whole of it, fare like my
        peers
    The heroes of old,
Bear the brunt, in a minute pay glad life's
        arrears
    Of pain, darkness and cold.
For sudden the worst turns the best to the brave
    The black minute's at end,
And the element's rage, the fiend-voices that
        rave,
    Shall dwindle, shall blend,
Shall change, shall become first a peace, then a
        joy,
    Then a light, then thy breast,
O thou soul of my soul !   I shall clasp thee again
    And with God be the rest !

THE SCHOLAR GIPSY   *Matthew*
                                                  Arnold

Go, for they call you, Shepherd, from the hill ;
    Go, Shepherd, and untie the wattled cotes :
        No longer leave thy wistful flock unfed,
    Nor let thy bawling fellows rack their throats,
        Nor the cropped grasses shoot another head.
            But when the fields are still,
        And the tired men and dogs all gone to rest,

And only the white sheep are sometimes
    seen
    Cross and recross the strips of moon-
      blanched green;
Come, Shepherd, and again renew the quest.

Here, where the reaper was at work of late,
    In this high field's dark corner, where he
      leaves
      His coat, his basket, and his earthen cruise,
And in the sun all morning binds the sheaves,
    Then here, at noon, comes back his stores
      to use;
      Here will I sit and wait,
    While to my ear from uplands far away
      The bleating of the folded flocks is borne,
      With distant cries of reapers in the corn—
All the live murmur of a summer's day.

Screened in this nook o'er the high, half-reaped
      field,
    And here till sundown, Shepherd, will I be.
      Through the thick corn the scarlet poppies
        peep.
    And round green roots and yellowing stalks
      I see
      Pale blue convolvulus in tendrils creep:
      And air-swept lindens yield
    Their scent, and rustle down their perfumed
      showers
      Of bloom on the bent grass where I am laid,
      And bower me from the August sun with
        shade;
    And the eye travels down to Oxford's towers:

And near me on the grass lies Glanvil's book— *Matthew*
  Come, let me read the oft-read tale again: *Arnold*
    The story of that Oxford scholar poor,
 Of pregnant parts and quick inventive brain,
     Who, tired of knocking at Preferment's door,
      One summer morn forsook
His friends, and went to learn the Gipsy lore,
    And roamed the world with that wild
      brotherhood,
    And came, as most men deemed, to little
      good,
But came to Oxford and his friends no more.

But once, years after, in the country lanes,
  Two scholars, whom at college erst he knew,
    Met him, and of his way of life enquired.
Whereat he answered that the Gipsy crew,
    His mates, had arts to rule as they desired
      The workings of men's brains;
And they can bind them to what thoughts they
      will:
    " And I," he said, " the secret of their art,
    When fully learned, will to the world impart:
But it needs Heaven-sent moments for this
     skill ! "

This said, he left them, and returned no more,
  But rumours hung about the country-side,
    That the lost Scholar long was seen to stray,
  Seen by rare glimpses, pensive and tongue-
      tied,
    In hat of antique shape, and cloak of grey,
     The same the Gipsies wore.
Shepherds had met him on the Hurst in spring;

*Matthew
Arnold*

At some lone alehouse in the Berkshire
      moors,
   On the warm ingle-bench, the smock-
      frocked boors
Had found him seated at their entering,

But, 'mid their drink and clatter, he would fly.
   And I myself seem half to know thy looks,
      And put the shepherds, Wanderer, on thy
         trace;
   And boys who in lone wheatfields scare the
      rooks
      I ask if thou hast passed their quiet place;
         Or in my boat I lie
Moored to the cool bank in the summer heats,
      'Mid wide grass meadows which the sun-
         shine fills,
      And watch the warm green-muffled Cumnor
         hills,
And wonder if thou haunt'st their shy retreats.

For most, I know, thou lov'st retired ground.
   Thee, at the ferry, Oxford riders blithe,
      Returning home on summer nights, have met
   Crossing the stripling Thames at Bablock-
         hithe,
      Trailing in the cool stream thy fingers wet,
         As the slow punt swings round:
   And leaning backwards in a pensive dream,
      And fostering in thy lap a heap of flowers
      Plucked in shy fields and distant Wychwood
         bowers,
   And thine eyes resting on the moonlit stream:

And then they land, and thou art seen no more. *Matthew*
  Maidens who from the distant hamlets come *Arnold*
    To dance around the Fyfield elm in May,
Oft through the darkening fields have seen thee
        roam,
      Or cross a stile into the public way.
        Oft thou hast given them store
  Of flowers—the frail-leafed, white anemone—
    Dark bluebells drenched with dews of
        summer eves,
      And purple orchises with spotted leaves—
But none has words she can report of thee.

And, above Godstow Bridge, when hay-time's
        here
  In June, and many a scythe in sunshine flames,
    Men who through those wide fields of
        breezy grass
  Where black-winged swallows haunt the
        glittering Thames,
      To bathe in the abandoned lasher pass,
        Have often passed thee near
  Sitting upon the river bank o'ergrown:
    Marked thine outlandish garb, thy figure
        spare,
    Thy dark vague eyes, and soft abstracted
        air;
  But, when they came from bathing, thou wert
        gone.

At some lone homestead in the Cumnor hills,
  Where at her open door the housewife darns,
    Thou hast been seen, or hanging on a gate
  To watch the threshers in the mossy barns.

Children, who early range these slopes and
late
For cresses from the rills,
Have known thee watching, all an April day,
The springing pastures and the feeding kine;
And marked thee, when the stars come out
and shine,
Through the long dewy grass move slow away.

In autumn, on the skirts of Bagley Wood,
Where most the Gipsies by the turf-edged way
Pitch their smoked tents, and every bush
you see
With scarlet patches tagged and shreds of grey,
Above the forest-ground called Thessaly—
The blackbird picking food
See thee, nor stops his meal, nor fears at all;
So often has he known thee past him stray
Rapt, twirling in thy hand a withered spray,
And waiting for the spark from Heaven to fall.

And once, in winter, on the causeway chill
Where home through flooded fields foot-
travellers go,
Have I not passed thee on the wooden bridge
Wrapt in thy cloak, and battling with the snow,
Thy face towards Hinksey and its wintry
ridge?
And thou hast climbed the hill
And gained the white brow of the Cumnor
range;
Turned once to watch, while thick snow-
flakes fall,

The line of festal light in Christ Church
hall—
Then sought thy straw in some sequestered
grange.

But what—I dream! Two hundred years are
flown
Since first thy story ran through Oxford halls,
And the grave Glanvil did the tale inscribe
That thou wert wandered from the studious
walls
To learn strange arts, and join a Gipsy tribe:
And thou from earth art gone
Long since, and in some quiet churchyard laid;
Some country nook, where o'er thy unknown
grave
Tall grasses and white flowering nettles
wave—
Under a dark red-fruited yew-tree's shade.

—No, no, thou hast not felt the lapse of hours.
For that wears out the life of mortal men?
'Tis that from change to change their being
rolls:
'Tis that repeated shocks, again, again,
Exhaust the energy of strongest souls,
And numb the elastic powers.
Till having used our nerves with bliss and teen,
And tired upon a thousand schemes our wit,
To the just-pausing Genius we remit
Our worn-out life, and are—what we have
been.

Matthew Arnold

Thou hast not lived, why shouldst thou perish,
    so ?
Thou hadst *one* aim, *one* business, *one* desire:
  Else wert thou long since numbered with the
    dead—
  Else hadst thou spent, like other men, thy fire.
    The generations of thy peers are fled,
      And we ourselves shall go;
  But thou possessest an immortal lot,
    And we imagine thee exempt from age
    And living as thou liv'st on Glanvil's page,
  Because thou hadst—what we, alas, have
    not !

For early didst thou leave the world, with powers
  Fresh, undiverted to the world without,
    Firm to their mark, not spent on other
      things;
  Free from the sick fatigue, the languid doubt,
    Which much to have tried, in much been
      baffled, brings.
     O Life unlike to ours !
  Who fluctuate idly without term or scope,
    Of whom each strives, nor knows for what
     he strives,
    And each half lives a hundred different
     lives;
  Who wait like thee, but not, like thee, in hope.

Thou waitest for the spark from Heaven: and
    we,
  Vague half-believers of our casual creeds,
    Who never deeply felt, nor clearly willed,
  Whose insight never has borne fruit in deeds,

Whose weak resolves never have been *Matthew*
    fulfilled;   *Arnold*
    For whom each year we see
Breeds new beginnings, disappointments new;
    Who hesitate and falter life away,
    And lose to-morrow the ground won to-
        day—
Ah, do not we, Wanderer, await it too?

Yes, we await it, but it still delays,
    And then we suffer; and amongst us One,
        Who most has suffered, takes dejectedly
His seat upon the intellectual throne;
        And all his store of sad experience he
        Lays bare of wretched days;
Tells us his misery's birth and growth and
        signs,
        And how the dying spark of hope was fed,
        And how the breast was soothed, and how
        the head,
And all his hourly varied anodynes.

This for our wisest: and we others pine,
    And wish the long unhappy dream would end,
        And waive all claim to bliss, and try to bear,
With close-lipped Patience for our only friend,
        Sad Patience, too near neighbour to Despair:
        But none has hope like thine.
Thou through the fields and through the wood
        dost stray,
        Roaming the country-side, a truant boy,
        Nursing thy project in unclouded joy,
And every doubt long blown by time away.

Matthew
Arnold

O born in days when wits were fresh and clear,
And life ran gaily as the sparkling Thames;
Before this strange disease of modern life,
With its sick hurry, its divided aims,
Its heads o'ertaxed, its palsied hearts, was
rife—
Fly hence, our contact fear!
Still fly, plunge deeper in the bowering wood!
Averse, as Dido did with gesture stern
From her false friend's approach in Hades
turn,
Wave us away, and keep thy solitude.

Still nursing the unconquerable hope,
Still clutching the inviolable shade,
With a free onward impulse brushing through
By night, the silvered branches of the glade—
Far on the forest skirts, where none pursue,
On some mild pastoral slope
Emerge, and resting on the moonlit pales,
Freshen thy flowers, as in former years,
With dew, or listen with enchanted ears,
From the dark dingles, to the nightingales.

But fly our paths, our feverish contact fly!
For strong the infection of our mental strife,
Which, though it gives no bliss, yet spoils
for rest;
And we should win thee from thy own fair
life,
Like us distracted, and like us unblest.
Soon, soon thy cheer would die,
Thy hopes grow timorous, and unfixed thy
powers,

And thy clear aims be cross and shifting
made:
And then thy glad perennial youth would
fade,
Fade, and grow old at last, and die like ours.

Then fly our greetings, fly our speech and smiles!
—As some grave Tyrian trader, from the sea,
Descried at sunrise an emerging prow
Lifting the cool-haired creepers stealthily,
The fringes of a southward-facing brow
Among the Ægean isles;
And saw the merry Grecian coaster come,
Freighted with amber grapes, and Chian
wine,
Green bursting figs, and tunnies steeped in
brine;
And knew the intruders on his ancient home,

The young light-hearted Masters of the waves;
And snatched his rudder, and shook out more
sail,
And day and night held on indignantly
O'er the blue Midland waters with the gale,
Betwixt the Syrtes and soft Sicily,
To where the Atlantic raves
Outside the Western Straits, and unbent sails
There, where down cloudy cliffs, through
sheets of foam,
Shy traffickers, the dark Iberians come;
And on the beach undid his corded bales.

A WISH

I ask not that my bed of death
From bands of greedy heirs be free;
For these besiege the latest breath
Of fortune's favoured sons, not me.

I ask not each kind soul to keep
Tearless, when of my death he hears.
Let those who will, if any, weep!
There are worse plagues on earth than tears.

I ask but that my death may find
The freedom to my life denied;
Ask but the folly of mankind
Then, then at last, to quit my side.

Spare me the whispering, crowded room,
The friends who come, and gape, and go;
The ceremonious air of gloom—
All which makes death a hideous show!

Nor bring, to see me cease to live,
Some doctor full of phrase and fame,
To shake his sapient head, and give
The ill he cannot cure a name.

Nor fetch, to take the accustomed toll
Of the poor sinner bound for death,
His brother-doctor of the soul,
To canvass with official breath

The future and its viewless things—
That undiscovered mystery
Which one who feels death's winnowing wings
Must need read clearer, sure, than he!

Bring none of these; but let me be,
While all around in silence lies,
Moved to the window near, and see
Once more, before my dying eyes,

Matthew Arnold

Bathed in the sacred dews of morn
The wide aerial landscape spread—
The world which was ere I was born,
The world which lasts when I am dead;

Which never was the friend of *one*,
Nor promised love it could not give,
But lit for all its generous sun,
And lived itself, and made us live.

There let me gaze, till I become
In soul, with what I gaze on, wed !
To feel the universe my home;
To have before my mind—instead

Of the sick-room, the mortal strife,
The turmoil for a little breath—
The pure eternal course of life,
Not human combatings with death !

Thus feeling, gazing, might I grow
Composed, refreshed, ennobled, clear;
Then willing let my spirit go
To work or wait elsewhere or here !

GROWING OLD

What is it to grow old ?
Is it to lose the glory of the form,
The lustre of the eye ?

Matthew Is it for Beauty to forego her wreath?
Arnold   Yes! but not this alone.

Is it to feel our strength—
Not our bloom only, but our strength—decay?
Is it to feel each limb
Grow stiffer, every function less exact,
Each nerve more weakly strung?

Yes! this, and more; but not,
Ah, 'tis not what in youth we dreamed 'twould
    be:
'Tis not to have our life
Mellowed and softened as with sunset-glow,
A golden day's decline.

'Tis not to see the world
As from a height, with rapt prophetic eyes
And heart profoundly stirred;
And weep, and feel the fulness of the past,
The years that are no more.

It is to spend long days
And not once feel that we were ever young;
It is to add, immured
In the hot prison of the present, month
To month with weary pain.

It is to suffer this,
And feel but half and feebly what we feel:
Deep in our hidden heart
Festers the dull remembrance of a change,
But no emotion,—none.

It is—last stage of all—
When we are frozen up within, and quite
The phantom of ourselves,
To hear the world applaud the hollow ghost
Which blamed the living man.

Matthew Arnold

THE BLESSED DAMOZEL

Dante Gabriel Rossetti

The blessed Damozel leaned out
    From the gold bar of Heaven;
Her eyes were deeper than the depth
    Of waters stilled at even;
She had three lilies in her hand,
    And the stars in her hair were seven.

Her robe, ungirt from clasp to hem,
    No wrought flowers did adorn,
But a white rose of Mary's gift
    For service meetly worn;
Her hair that lay along her back,
    Was yellow like ripe corn.

Herseemed she scarce had been a day
    One of God's choristers;
The wonder was not yet quite gone
    From that still look of hers;
Albeit, to them she left, her day
    Had counted as ten years.

(To one it is ten years of years:
    . . . Yet now, here in this place,
Surely she leaned o'er me,—her hair
    Fell all about my face. . . .

Nothing: the autumn-fall of leaves.
   The whole year sets apace.)

     It was the rampart of God's house
      That she was standing on;
By God built over the sheer depth
  In which is Space begun;
So high, that looking downward thence,
  She scarce could see the sun.

It lies in Heaven across the flood
  Of ether, as a bridge.
Beneath, the tides of day and night
  With flame and darkness ridge
The void, as low as where his earth
  Spins like a fretful midge.

Around her, lovers, newly met
  'Mid deathless love's acclaims,
Spoke evermore among themselves,
  Their heart-remembered names;
And the souls, mounting up to God,
  Went by her like thin flames.

And still she bowed herself, and stooped
  Out of the circling charm;
Until her bosom must have made
  The bar she leaned on warm,
And the lilies lay as if asleep
  Along her bended arm.

From the fixed place of Heaven, she saw
  Time, like a pulse, shake fierce
Through all the worlds.   Her gaze still strove,
  Within the gulf to pierce

Its path; and now she spoke as when
   The stars sang in their spheres.

*Dante
Gabriel
Rossetti*

The sun was gone now; the curled moon
   Was like a little feather
Fluttering far down the gulf; and now
   She spoke through the still weather,
Her voice was like the voice the stars
   Had when they sang together.

(Ah sweet ! Even now in that bird's song,
   Strove not her accents there,
Fain to be hearkened ? When those bells
   Possessed the mid-day air,
Strove not her steps to reach my side
   Down all the echoing stair ?)

" I wish that he were come to me,
   For he will come," she said.
" Have I not prayed in Heaven ? on earth
   Lord, Lord, has he not prayed ?
Are not two prayers a perfect strength ?
   And shall I feel afraid ?

" When round his head the aureole clings,
   And he is clothed in white,
I'll take his hand and go with him
   To the deep wells of light;
As unto a stream we will step down,
   And bathe there in God's sight.

" We two will stand beside that shrine,
   Occult, withheld, untrod,
Whose lamps are stirred continually
   With prayer sent up to God;
And see our old prayers granted, melt
   Each like a little cloud.

Dante
Gabriel
Rossetti "We two will lie i' the shadow of
   That living mystic tree
Within whose secret growth the Dove
   Is sometimes felt to be,
While every leaf that His plumes touch
   Saith His Name audibly.

"And I myself will teach to him
   I myself, lying so,
The songs I sing here; which his voice
   Shall pause in, hushed and slow,
And find some knowledge at each pause,
   Or some new thing to know."

(Alas! we two, we two, thou say'st!
   Yea, one wast thou with me
That once of old.   But shall God lift
   To endless unity
The soul whose likeness with thy soul
   Was but its love for thee?)

"We two," she said, "will seek the groves
   Where the lady Mary is,
With her five handmaidens, whose names
   Are five sweet symphonies:—
Cecily, Gertrude, Magdalen,
   Margaret and Rosalys.

"Circlewise sit they, with bound locks
   And foreheads garlanded;
Into the fine cloth white like flame,
   Weaving the golden thread,
To fashion the birth-robes for them
   Who are just born, being dead.

"He shall fear, haply, and be dumb:
  Then I will lay my cheek
To his, and tell about our love,
  Not once abashed or weak:
And the dear Mother will approve
  My pride, and let me speak.

*Dante
Gabriel
Rossetti*

"Herself shall bring us, hand in hand,
  To Him round whom all souls
Kneel, the clear-ranged unnumbered heads
  Bowed with their aureoles:
And angels, meeting us, shall sing
  To their citherns and citoles.

"There will I ask of Christ the Lord
  Thus much for him and me:—
Only to live as once on earth
  With Love,—only to be,
As then awhile, for ever now
  Together, I and he."

She gazed, and listened, and then said,
  Less sad of speech than mild,—
"All this is when he comes."   She ceased.
  The light thrilled towards her, filled
With angels, in strong level lapse.
  Her eyes prayed, and she smiled.

(I saw her smile.)   But soon their path
  Was vague in distant spheres.
And then she cast her arms along
  The golden barriers,
And laid her face between her hands,
  And wept.   (I heard her tears.)

111

*Dante
Gabriel
Rossetti*

Think thou and act; tomorrow thou shalt die.
Outstretched in the sun's warmth upon the shore,
Thou say'st: " Man's measured path is all gone
    o'er:
Up all his years, steeply, with strain and sigh,
Men clomb until he touched the truth; and I,
Even I, am he whom it was destined for."
How should this be? Art thou then so much
    more
Than they who sowed, that thou shouldst reap
    thereby?

Nay, come up hither. From this wave-washed
    mound
Unto the furthest flood-brim look with me;
Then reach on with thy thought till it be
    drowned.
Miles and miles distant though the last line be,
And though thy soul sail leagues and leagues
    beyond,—
Still, leagues beyond those leagues, there is more
    sea.

WITHOUT HER

What of her glass without her? The blank grey
There where the pool is blind of the moon's face.
Her dress without her? The tossed empty
    space

Of cloud-rack whence the moon has passed *Dante*
    away.   *Gabriel*
Her paths without her ?   Day's appointed sway *Rossetti*
Usurped by desolate night.   Her pillowed place
Without her ?   Tears, ah me ! for love's good
    grace,
And cold forgetfulness of night or day.

What of the heart without her ?   Nay, poor
    heart,
Of thee what word remains ere speech be still ?
A wayfarer by barren ways and chill,
Steep ways and weary, without her thou art,
Where the long cloud, the long wood's counter-
    part,
Sheds doubled darkness up the labouring hill.

LOST DAYS

The lost days of my life until today,
What were they, could I see them on the street
Lie as they fell ?   Would they be ears of wheat
Sown once for food but trodden into clay ?
Or golden coins squandered and still to pay ?
Or drops of blood dabbling the guilty feet ?
Or such spilt water as in dreams must cheat
The undying throats of Hell, athirst alway ?

I do not see them here ; but after death
God knows I know the faces I shall see,
Each one a murdered self, with low last breath,
" I am thyself,—what hast thou done to me ? "
" And I—and I—thyself," (lo ! each one saith,)
" And thou thyself to all eternity ! "

THE HONEYSUCKLE

I plucked a honeysuckle where
    The hedge on high is quick with thorn,
    And, climbing for the prize, was torn,
And fouled my feet in quag-water;
    And by the thorns and by the wind
    The blossom that I took was thinned,
And yet I found it sweet and fair.

Thence to a richer growth I came,
    Where, nursed in mellow intercourse,
    The honeysuckles sprang by scores,
Not harried like my single stem,
    All virgin lamps of scent and dew.
    So from my hand that first I threw,
Yet plucked not any more of them.

THE WOODSPURGE

The wind flapped loose, the wind was still,
Shaken out dead from tree and hill.
I had walked on at the wind's will,—
I sat now, for the wind was still.

Between my knees my forehead was,—
My lips, drawn in, said not Alas!
My hair was over in the grass,
My naked ears heard the day pass.

My eyes, wide open, had the run
Of some ten weeds to fix upon;
Among those few, out of the sun,
The woodspurge flowered, three cups in one.

From perfect grief there need not be
Wisdom or even memory:
One thing then learnt remains to me,—
The woodspurge has a cup of three.

Dante Gabriel Rossetti

"THERE WAS A CHILD WENT FORTH..." *Walt Whitman*

There was a child went forth every day,
And the first object he looked upon, that object
he became,
And that object became part of him for the day,
or a certain part of the day,
Or for many years or stretching cycles of years.

The early lilacs became part of this child,
And grass, and white and red morning-glories,
and white and red clover, and the song of
the phœbe-bird,
And the Third-month lambs, and the sow's pink-
faint litter, and the mare's foal and the cow's
calf.
And the noisy brood of the barn-yard, or by the
mire of the pond-side,
And the fish suspending themselves so curiously
below there—and the beautiful curious
liquid,
And the water-plants with their graceful flat
heads—all became part of him.

The field-sprouts of Fourth-month and Fifth-
month became part of him;
Winter-grain sprouts, and those of the light-
yellow corn, and the esculent roots of the
garden,
And the apple-trees covered with blossoms, and
the fruit afterwards, and wood-berries, and
the commonest weeds by the road;
And the old drunkard staggering home from the
outhouse of the tavern, whence he had
lately risen,
And the schoolmistress that passed on her way
to the school,
And the friendly boys that passed—and the
quarrelsome boys,
And the tidy and fresh-cheeked girls—and the
barefoot negro boy and girl,
And all the changes of city and country, wherever
he went.

His own parents,
He that had fathered him and she that had
conceived him in her womb and birthed
him,
They gave this child more of themselves than
that,
They gave him afterward every day—they
became part of him.
The mother at home, quietly placing the dishes
on the supper-table;
The mother with mild words—clean her cap and
gown, a wholesome odour falling off her
person and clothes as she walks by;

116

The father, strong, self-sufficient, manly, mean, *Walt*
    angered, unjust;   *Whitman*
The blow, the quick loud word, the tight bargain,
    the crafty lure,
The family usages, the language, the company,
    the furniture—the yearning and swelling
    heart,
Affection that will not be gainsayed—the sense
    of what is real—the thought if after all it
    should prove unreal,
The doubts of day-time and the doubts of
    night-time—the curious whether and
    how,
Whether that which appears so is so, or is it all
    flashes and specks?
Men and women crowding fast in the streets—
    if they are not flashes and specks, what are
    they?
The streets themselves, and the façades of houses
    and goods in the windows,
Vehicles, teams, the heavy-planked wharves—
    the huge crossing at the ferries,
The village on the highland seen from afar at
    sunset—the river between,
Shadows, aureola and mist, the light falling on
    roofs and gables of white or brown, three
    miles off,
The schooner near by, sleepily dropping down
    the tide—the little boat slack-towed astern,
The hurrying tumbling waves, quick-broken
    crests, slapping,
The strata of coloured clouds, the long bar of
    maroon tint, away solitary by itself—the
    spread of purity it lies motionless in,

*Walt
Whitman*
The horizon's edge, the flying sea-crow, the
  fragrance of salt marsh and shore mud;
These became part of that child who went forth
  every day, and who now goes, and will
  always go forth every day.

"AS I LAY WITH MY HEAD IN YOUR LAP, CAMERADO . . ."

As I lay with my head in your lap, Camerado,
The confession I made I resume—what I said to
  you in the open air I resume:
I know I am restless, and make others so;
I know my words are weapons, full of danger,
  full of death;
For I confront peace, security, and all the settled
  laws, to unsettle them;
I am more resolute because all have denied me,
  than I could ever have been had all accepted
  me;
I heed not, and have never heeded *either* experience, cautions, majorities, *or* ridicule;
And the threat of what is called hell is little or
  nothing to me;
And the lure of what is called heaven is little or
  nothing to me;
Dear Camerado! I confess I have urged you
  onward with me, and still urge you, without
  the least idea what is our destination,
Or whether we shall be victorious, or utterly
  quelled and defeated.

118

*Walt
Whitman*

I need no assurances—I am a man who is pre-
    occupied of his own Soul;
I do not doubt that from under the feet, and
    beside the hands and face I am cognizant
    of, are now looking faces I am not cog-
    nizant of—calm and actual faces;
I do not doubt but the majesty and beauty of the
    world are latent in any iota of the world;
I do not doubt I am limitless, and that the uni-
    verses are limitless—in vain I try to think
    how limitless;
I do not doubt that the orbs, and the systems of
    orbs, play their swift sports through the air
    on purpose—and that I shall one day be
    eligible to do as much as they, and more
    than they;
I do not doubt that temporary affairs keep on
    and on, millions of years;
I do not doubt interiors have their interiors, and
    exteriors have their exteriors—and that the
    eyesight has another eyesight, and the hear-
    ing another hearing, and the voice another
    voice;
I do not doubt that the passionately-wept deaths
    of young men are provided for—and that
    the deaths of young women, and the deaths
    of little children, are provided for,
(Did you think Life was so well provided for—
    and Death, the purport of all Life, is not
    well provided for?)

I do not doubt that wrecks at sea, no matter
      what the horrors of them—no matter whose
      wife, child, husband, father, lover, has gone
      down, are provided for, to the minutest
      points;
I do not doubt that whatever can possibly
      happen, anywhere, at any time, is provided
      for, in the inherences of things;
I do not think Life provides for all, and for Time
      and Space—but I believe Heavenly Death
      provides for all.

"WHEN I PERUSE THE CONQUERED
FAME ..."

When I peruse the conquered fame of heroes,
      and the victories of mighty generals, I do
      not envy the generals,
Nor the President in his Presidency, nor the rich
      in his great house;
But when I hear of the brotherhood of lovers,
      how it was with them,
How through life, through dangers, odium, un-
      changing, long and long,
Through youth, and through middle and old
      age, how unfaltering, how affectionate and
      faithful they were,
Then I am pensive—I hastily walk away filled
      with the bitterest envy.

As I sit with others, at a great feast, suddenly,
    while the music is playing,
To my mind, (whence it comes I know not,)
    spectral, in mist, of a wreck at sea;
Of certain ships—how they sail from port with
    flying streamers, and wafted kisses—and
    that is the last of them!
Of the solemn and murky mystery about the
    fate of the *President*;
Of the flower of the marine science of fifty
    generations, foundered off the Northeast
    coast and going down—Of the steamship
    Arctic going down,
Of the veiled tableau—women gathered together
    on deck, pale, heroic, waiting the moment
    that draws so close—O the moment!
A huge sob—a few bubbles—the white foam
    spirting up—and then the women gone,
Sinking there, while the passionless wet flows on
    —And I now pondering, Are those women
    indeed gone?
Are souls drowned and destroyed so?
Is only matter triumphant?

THE LAST INVOCATION

At the last, tenderly,
From the walls of the powerful, fortressed house
From the clasp of the knitted locks—from the
    keep of the well-closed doors,
Let me be wafted.

Walt
Whitman
Let me glide noiselessly forth;
With the key of softness unlock the locks—with
   a whisper,
Set ope the doors, O Soul !

Tenderly ! be not impatient,
(Strong is your hold, O mortal flesh !
Strong is your hold, O love!)

James
Thomson
From THE CITY OF DREADFUL NIGHT

I

Because he seemed to walk with an intent
   I followed him; who, shadowlike and frail,
Unswervingly though slowly onward went,
   Regardless, wrapt in thought as in a veil:
Thus step for step with lonely sounding feet
We travelled many a long dim silent street.

At length he paused: a black mass in the gloom,
   A tower that merged into the heavy sky;
Around, the huddled stones of grave and tomb:
   Some old God's-acre now corruption's sty:
He murmured to himself with dull despair,
Here Faith died, poisoned by this charnel air.

Then turning to the right went on once more,
   And travelled weary roads without suspense;
And reached at last a low wall's open door,
   Whose villa gleamed beyond the foliage dense:
He gazed, and muttered with a hard despair,
Here Love died, stabbed by its own worshipped
      pair.

Then turning to the right resumed his march,   *James*
   And travelled streets and lanes with wondrous *Thomson*
      strength,
Until on stooping through a narrow arch
   We stood before a squalid house at length:
He gazed, and whispered with a cold despair,
Here Hope died, starved out in its utmost lair.

When he had spoken thus, before he stirred,
   I spoke, perplexed by something in the signs
Of desolation I had seen and heard
   In this drear pilgrimage to ruined shrines:
When Faith and Love and Hope are dead indeed
Can Life still live? By what doth it proceed?

As whom his one intense thought overpowers,
   He answered coldly, Take a watch, erase
The signs and figures of the circling hours,
   Detach the hands, remove the dial-face;
The works proceed until run down; although
Bereft of purpose, void of use, still go.

II

As I came through the desert thus it was,
As I came through the desert: Eyes of fire
Glared at me throbbing with a starved desire;
The hoarse and heavy and carnivorous breath
Was hot upon me from deep jaws of death;
Sharp claws, swift talons, fleshless fingers cold
Plucked at me from the bushes, tried to hold:
         But I strode on austere;
         No hope could have no fear.

James Thomson As I came through the desert thus it was,
As I came through the desert: Lo you, there,
That hillock burning with a brazen glare;
Those myriad dusky flames with points a-glow
Which writhed and hissed and darted to and fro;

A Sabbath of the Serpents, heaped pell-mell
For Devil's roll-call and some fête of Hell:
      Yet I strode on austere;
      No hope could have no fear.

As I came through the desert thus it was,
As I came through the desert: Meteors ran
And crossed their javelins on the black sky-
    span;
The zenith opened to a gulf of flame,
The dreadful thunderbolts jarred earth's fixed
    frame;
The ground all heaved in waves of fire that surged
And weltered round me sole there unsubmerged:
      Yet I strode on austere;
      No hope could have no fear.

As I came through the desert thus it was,
As I came through the desert: Air once more,
And I was close upon a wild sea-shore;
Enormous cliffs arose on either hand.
The deep tide thundered up a league-broad
    strand;
White foambelts seethed there, wan spray swept
    and flew;
The sky broke, moon and stars and clouds and
    blue:
      And I strode on austere;
      No hope could have no fear.

As I came through the desert thus it was,   *James*
As I came through the desert: On the left   *Thomson*
The sun arose and crowned a broad crag-cleft;
There stopped and burned out black, except a
    rim,
A bleeding eyeless socket, red and dim;
Whereon the moon fell suddenly south-west,
And stood above the right-hand cliffs at rest:
       Still I strode on austere;
       No hope could have no fear.

HERACLITUS

*William
Johnson
Cory*

They told me, Heraclitus, they told me you were
    dead,
They brought me bitter news to hear and bitter
    tears to shed.
I wept as I remembered how often you and I
Had tired the sun with talking and sent him
    down the sky.

And now that thou art lying, my dear old Carian
    guest,
A handful of grey ashes, long, long ago at rest,
Still are thy pleasant voices, thy nightingales,
    awake;
For Death, he taketh all away, but them he
    cannot take.

How long shall men deny the flower
   Because its roots are in the earth,
And crave with tears from God the dower
   They have, and have despised as dearth,
And scorn as low their human lot,
   With frantic pride, too blind to see
That standing on the head makes not
   Either for ease or dignity !
But fools shall feel like fools to find
   (Too late informed) that angels' mirth
Is one in cause, and mode, and kind
   With that which they profaned on earth.

THE REVELATION

An idle poet, here and there,
   Looks round him; but, for all the rest,
The world, unfathomably fair,
   Is duller than a witling's jest.
Love wakes men, once a lifetime each;
   They lift their heavy lids, and look;
And, lo, what one sweet page can teach,
   They read with joy, then shut the book.
And some give thanks, and some blaspheme,
   And most forget; but, either way,
That and the Child's unheeded dream
   Is all the light of all their day.

MAGNA EST VERITAS

*Coventry
Patmore*

Here, in this little bay,
Full of tumultuous life and great repose,
Where, twice a day,
The purposeless, glad ocean comes and goes,
Under high cliffs, and far from the huge town,
I sit me down.
For want of me the world's course will not fail:
When all its work is done, the lie shall rot;
The truth is great and shall prevail,
When none cares whether it prevail or not.

A BIRTHDAY

*Christina
Rossetti*

My heart is like a singing bird
  Whose nest is in a watered shoot;
My heart is like an apple-tree
  Whose boughs are bent with thickset fruit;
My heart is like a rainbow shell
  That paddles in a halcyon sea;
My heart is gladder than all these,
  Because my love is come to me.

Raise me a daïs of silk and down;
  Hang it with vair and purple dyes;
Carve it in doves and pomegranates,
  And peacocks with a hundred eyes;
Work it in gold and silver grapes,
  In leaves, and silver fleurs-de-lys;
Because the birthday of my life
  Is come, my love is come to me.

THE ONE CERTAINTY

Christina Rossetti

Vanity of vanities, the Preacher saith,
All things are vanity.   The eye and ear
Cannot be filled with what they see and hear.
Like early dew, or like the sudden breath
Of wind, or like the grass that withereth,
Is man, tossed to and fro by hope and fear:
So little joy hath he, so little cheer,
Till all things end in the long dust of death.
To-day is still the same as yesterday,
To-morrow also even as one of them;
And there is nothing new under the sun:
Until the ancient race of Time be run,
The old thorns shall grow out of the old stem,
And morning shall be cold and twilight grey.

REST

O earth, lie heavily upon her eyes;
Seal her sweet eyes weary of watching, Earth;
Lie close around her; leave no room for mirth
With its harsh laughter, nor for sound of sighs.
She hath no questions, she hath no replies,
Hushed in and curtained with a blessed dearth
Of all that irked her from the hour of birth;
With stillness that is almost Paradise.
Darkness more clear than noon-day holdeth
     her,
Silence more musical than any song;
Even her very heart has ceased to stir:
Until the morning of Eternity
Her rest shall not begin nor end, but be;
And when she wakes she will not think it long.

AMEN

*Christina
Rossetti*

It is over.   What is over?
  Nay, how much is over truly!—
Harvest days we toiled to sow for;
  Now the sheaves are gathered newly,
  Now the wheat is garnered duly.

It is finished.   What is finished?
  Much is finished known or unknown:
Lives are finished; time diminished;
  Was the fallow field left unsown?
  Will these buds be always unblown?

It suffices.   What suffices?
  All suffices reckoned rightly:
Spring shall bloom where now the ice is,
  Roses make the bramble sightly,
  And the quickening sun shine brightly,
  And the latter wind blow lightly,
And my garden teem with spices.

PASSING AWAY

Passing away, saith the World, passing away:
Chances, beauty and youth sapped day by day:
Thy life never continueth in one stay.
Is the eye waxen dim, is the dark hair changing
    to grey
That hath won neither laurel nor bay?
I shall clothe myself in Spring and bud in May:
Thou, root-stricken, shalt not rebuild thy decay
On my bosom for aye.
Then I answered: Yea.

E—I 129

Christina
Rossetti

Passing away, saith my Soul, passing away:
With its burden of fear and hope, of labour and
    play,
Hearken what the past doth witness and say:
Rust in thy gold, a moth is in thine array,
A canker is in thy bud, thy leaf must decay.
At midnight, at cockcrow, at morning, one
    certain day,
Lo, the Bridegroom shall come and shall not
    delay:
Watch thou and pray.
Then I answered: Yea.

Passing away, saith my God, passing away:
Winter passeth after the long delay:
New grapes on the vine, new figs on the tender
    spray,
Turtle calleth turtle in Heaven's May.
Though I tarry, wait for me, trust me, watch and
    pray.
Arise, come away; night is past, and lo, it is day;
My love, my sister, my spouse, thou shalt hear
    me say—
Then I answered: Yea.

SILENCES

Arthur
O'Shaugh-
nessy

'Tis a world of silences.   I gave a cry
In the first sorrow my heart could not withstand;
I saw men pause, and listen, and look sad,
As though an answer in their hearts they had;

Some turned away, some came and took my
   hand,
        For all reply.

I stood beside a grave.   Years had passed by;
Sick with unanswered life I turned to death,
And whispered all my question to the grave,
And watched the flowers desolately wave,
And grass stir on it with a fitful breath,
        For all reply.

I raised my eyes to heaven; my prayer went high
Into the luminous mystery of the blue;
My thought of God was purer than a flame
And God it seemed a little nearer came,
Then passed; and greater still the silence grew,
        For all reply.

By you !   If I can speak before I die,
I spoke to you with all my soul, and when
I look at you 'tis still my soul you see.
Oh, in your heart was there no word for me ?
All would have answered had you answered then
        With even a sigh.

SONG

I went to her who loveth me no more,
And prayed her bear with me, if so she might;
For I had found day after day too sore,
And tears that would not cease night after night.
And so I prayed her, weeping, that she bore

To let me be with her a little; yea,
To soothe myself a little with her sight,
Who loved me once, ah ! many a night and day.

Then she who loveth me no more, maybe
She pitied somewhat ! and I took a chain
To bind myself to her, and her to me ;
Yea, so that I might call her mine again.
Lo ! she forbade me not: but I and she
Fettered her fair limbs, and her neck more fair,
Chained the fair wasted white of love's domain,
And put gold fetters on her golden hair.

Oh ! the vain joy it is to see her lie
Beside me once again; beyond release,
Her hair, her hand, her body, till she die,
All mine, for me to do with as I please !
For, after all, I find no chain whereby
To chain her heart to love me as before,
Nor fetter for her lips, to make them cease
From saying still she loveth me no more.

Lord
de Tabley
THE COUNT OF SENLIS AT HIS TOILET

What scrap is this, you thrust upon me now ?
Some grievance-bill; I'm sick of seeing such.
What can these burghers always want with
    me ?
I am weary of petitions, yet they pour.
This is a brave word, liberty, indeed ;
And nowadays each lean and mongrel whelp
Littered about these streets chimes in his voice

132

For liberty. I loathe the letters' sound.
How dare you bring this in at 'tiring time,
Fretting my soul?   This chain is dull as
      brass,
Lean down you caitiff, lacquer up the gold;
Rub for your life, rub.   There's another stone
Flawed in the centre droplet, where it shows,
Cracked like a nut; why, man, it was a gem,
An amethyst as clear as a girl's eye.
And you must crash my chain about like sacks
Of Kathern pears; there are no servants, none,
As I remember service, in these days;
A new time pestilent; each clown must ride
And nobles trudge behind him in the dirt—
Lay out my murrey-coloured velvet suit:
How you detain me fumbling; knave and fool,
Don't ruffle back the pile of Genoa's looms
With your rank sweating fingers the wrong way.
Do you suppose I wear a wild-cat's fur
For your amusement? You must play these
      tricks,
With only half-an-hour to banquet time;
And when I rail, stand helpless, gibbering there,
As if a nobleman could tire himself
Like a field scare-crow against time and grain,
You'd have me round my shoulders toss a
      sack,
And give my hair one shake, and make an end,
And so stride in among the grey-green eyes,
And dainty hands, and little perfumed arms,
And white smooth laughing kittens at their
      play;
Dear hearts, I think they call it love-making,
A purr begins it and a scratching ends,

Or each succeeds alternate; bless them all:
You, with these darlings waiting, prove a snail.
Your careless hands would send me to the feast
Slimed in disorder.   You've the mind, it seems,
And leisure to disgrace me.   Try, my knave.
You that are born upon my liberties,
And I've the right of gibbet on my lands,
At least my fathers had it, that's the same;
If time is able to filch lawful rights
Away from any man without his leave,
Then let time void the ducats from my pouch,
When I refuse to spend them.   Have then heed.
And now this gentle rabble, that I own,
Have bribed you here, my thrall, to bring me in
A string of rank seditions on a rag
Of calfskin, at the very time and hour
You know, it chiefly sets me out of gear
To find thus rudely thrust beneath my nose
The wrongs of carrion butchers, the sweet sighs
Of carters, longing after equal laws.
To push these in of all the hours of the day,
To vex me here half-dressed, is shameless
          deed,
Consider only, certain moments hence
The banquet summons finds me, pest of
          heaven !
With my mind ruffled, half my clothes awry;
I'm sent among damsels at the board,
With a sour taste of serfdom in my mouth;
I am put from my whole amenity;
My pleasing power and courteous manner lost;
For such light sunny ways will not beam out,
Unless I can forget, ignore, abolish,
The sweating boors penned in their styes below.

Man, man, is this a time for wrong and right ? *Lord*
The doublet bulges, the ruff hangs awry,   *de Tabley*
Limp as the wool of some damp wether's fleece.
The feast is ready—they are going down,—
I hear Count Edmund, coxcomb, on the stairs—
You loiter, varlet, and I'm late; your deed;
You thrust your charters when I ought to dress;
Charters indeed.   I that have known it long,
Have never seen this precious burgh of mine
Save on the eve of starving thro' my dues,
At least their song has run so all these years,
And yet they are fed enough to roar out loud,
" Behold, we starve ! " —My ruffles; that's the
          left,
You idiot—and they breed too, breed like rats;
So much the better for my toll per head.
They will not starve; I'd like to see it done.
They can cheat hunger in a hundred ways;
They rob my saw-pits clean of bran for bread;
There never were such greedy knaves as these.
They clear my outer court of nettles next;
They boil them, so I'm told; I hope they sting
Well, I shall not complain, it saves the scythe,
And we great lords must wink and let ourselves
Be pilfered by the small fry halter ripe.
It is the doom and meed of noble blood
To be a prey to clowns; and God, He knows,
I am not one of those who grudge the poor.
And so my kindness fills them full of corn,
And rains this plague down in petitions thus.
I am soft hearted, they presume on this—
And I will singe clean out your fishy eyes
With white-hot tongs, unless you make that
          cloak

135

Lord
de Tabley Fall smoother on the carriage of my sword.
Why, you lean hound, whom mange will soon destroy
And save your hanging, where's the scabbard brace?
See, you have made it stick right out behind
Like Satan's sister's broomstick.   And the cooks
Are at it dishing up.   You fumble there,
As if the precious minutes stood like sheep,
And you'd the day to lie upon the grass
And count the crows.   There, that goes better—Come,
I'll glance on this petition—What is here?
" That our starvation is no idle tale,
Of his own seeing our liege lord must know;
Since his own noble and peculiar pack
In tufted sedges at the mort o' the deer,
Lately unearthed a lean white woman dead."—
Confound the knaves; and granting this were so,
This is a delicate and savoury thing
Just before dinner to remind me of.
This shall spoil all I meant to do for them;
How dare they? Why this same wan rigid face
Must thrust itself upon my grounds and die,
And sicken several pretty damsels found,
And spoil the hunting of a score of lords;
And damp the show.   No wonder; I myself
Felt rather squeamish half a dial's turn,
And found strong waters needful to reset
The impassive mettle of high breeding's ways.
And then my Kate, who'll laugh a lawyer dumb,
Was all that evening dull as a town clock;

And later on—here catch this trash—a word *Lord*
More and I clap a double impost on, *de Tabley*
And make them starve in earnest.   Tell them so,
Sir thief, my varlet, their ambassador.—
Enough of this, why drivel we on these ?
Get, for Saint Job's sake, forward with my beard.
You push this trivial business in my jowl,
And make me dawdle over urgent cares,
And tice me to peruse, while your rough hands
Will turn me out a Scythian for the feast,
In barbarous disorder.   Is that all ?
My ring and gloves;—Count Edmund, there he
    goes;
How that fool brags about his pedigree;
His veins must run pure ichor, ours mere blood.
I'd gladly try my rapier on his ribs,
And bleed him much as any plough-boy bleeds.
How can a man speak any such vain words ?—
I hear him swinging down the corridor,
With all his plumage and bedizened hide
As clean as a cobswan's—trust him for that—
He has no thought above his skin and gloves,
Or at what angle his trim beard should grow;
Despatch, thou slave; complete me, or indeed
He'll be before me with the duchess yet.

THE KNIGHT IN THE WOOD

The thing itself was rough and crudely done,
Cut in coarse stone, spitefully placed aside
As merest lumber, where the light was worst,
On a back staircase.   Overlooked it lay
In a great Roman palace crammed with art.

It has no number in the list of gems,
Weeded away long since, pushed out and
    banished,
Before insipid Guidos over-sweet,
And Dolce's rare sensationalities,
And curly chirping angels spruce as birds.
And yet the motive of this thing ill-hewn
And hardly seen *did* touch me. O, indeed,
The skill-less hand that carved it had belonged
To a most yearning and bewildered heart,
There was such desolation in its work;
And through its utter failure the thing spoke
With more of human message, heart to heart,
Than all these faultless, smirking, skin-deep
    saints;
In artificial troubles picturesque,
And martyred sweetly, not one curl awry.—
Listen; a clumsy knight who rode alone
Upon a stumbling jade in a great wood
Belated. The poor beast with head low-bowed
Snuffing the treacherous ground. The rider leant
Forward to sound the marish with his lance.
You saw the place was deadly; that doomed pair,
The wretched rider and the hide-bound steed
Feared to advance, feared to return—That's all.

MISREPRESENTATION

Peace, there is nothing more for men to speak;
A larger wisdom than our lips' decrees.
Of that dumb mouth no longer reason seek,
No censure reaches that eternal peace,
    And that immortal ease.

Believe them not that would disturb the end
With earth's invidious comment, idly meant.
Speak and have done thy evil; for my friend
Is gone beyond all human discontent,
      And wisely went.

Say what you will and have your sneer and go.
You see the specks, we only heed the fruit
Of a great life, whose truth—men hate truth so—
No lukewarm age of compromise could suit.
      Laugh and be mute?

*Lord
de Tabley*

OLD LOVE

*William
Morris*

" You must be very old, Sir Giles,"
  I said; he said: " Yea, very old ! "
Whereat the mournfullest of smiles
  Creased his dry skin with many a fold.

" They hammered out my basnet point
  Into a round salade," he said,
" The basnet being quite out of joint,
  Natheless the salade rasps my head."

He gazed at the great fire awhile:
  " And you are getting old, Sir John; "
(He said this with that cunning smile
  That was most sad): " we both wear on;

" Knights come to court and look at me,
  With eyebrows up; except my lord,
And my dear lady, none I see
  That knows the ways of my old sword."

(My lady ! at that word no pang
    Stopped all my blood.)   " But tell me, John,
Is it quite true that pagans hang
    So thick about the east, that on

" The eastern sea no Venice flag
    Can fly unpaid for ? " " True," I said,
" And in such way the miscreants drag
    Christ's cross upon the ground, I dread

" That Constantine must fall this year."
    Within my heart: " These things are small;
This is not small, that things outwear
    I thought were made for ever, yea, all.

" All things go soon or late," I said.
    I saw the duke in court next day;
Just as before, his grand great head
    Above his gold robes dreaming lay,

Only his face was paler; there
    I saw his duchess sit by him;
And she—she was changed more; her hair
    Before my eyes that used to swim,

And make me dizzy with great bliss,
    Once, when I used to watch her sit—
Her hair is bright still, yet it is
    As though some dust were thrown on it.

Her eyes are shallower, as though
    Some grey glass were behind; her brow
And cheeks the straining bones show through,
    Are not so good for kissing now.

Her lips are drier now she is
  A great duke's wife these many years,
They will not shudder with a kiss
  As once they did, being moist with tears.

*William
Morris*

Also her hands have lost that way
  Of clinging that they used to have;
They looked quite easy, as they lay
  Upon the silken cushions brave

With broidery of the apples green
  My Lord Duke bears upon his shield.
Her face, alas! that I have seen
  Look fresher than an April field,

This is all gone now; gone also
  Her tender walking; when she walks
She is most queenly I well know,
  And she is fair still:—As the stalks

Of faded summer-lilies are,
  So is she grown now unto me
This spring-time, when the flowers star
  The meadows, birds sing wonderfully.

I warrant once she used to cling
  About his neck, and kissed him so,
And then his coming step would ring
  Joy-bells for her,—some time ago.

Ah! sometimes like an idle dream
  That hinders true life overmuch,
Sometimes like a lost heaven, these seem—
  This love is not so hard to smutch.

Had she come all the way for this,
To part at last without a kiss?
Yea, had she borne the dirt and rain
That her own eyes might see him slain
Beside the haystack in the floods?

Along the dripping leafless woods,
The stirrup touching either shoe,
She rode astride as troopers do;
With kirtle kilted to her knee,
To which the mud splashed wretchedly;
And the wet dripped from every tree
Upon her head and heavy hair,
And on her eyelids broad and fair;
The tears and rain ran down her face.

By fits and starts they rode apace,
And very often was his place
Far off from her; he had to ride
Ahead, to see what might betide
When the roads crossed; and sometimes, when
There rose a murmuring from his men,
Had to turn back with promises;
Ah me! she had but little ease;
And often for pure doubt and dread
She sobbed, made giddy in the head
By the swift riding; while, for cold,
Her slender fingers scarce could hold
The wet reins; yea, and scarcely, too,
She felt the foot within her shoe
Against the stirrup: all for this,
To part at last without a kiss
Beside the haystack in the floods.

For when they neared that rain-soaked hay, *William*
They saw across the only way *Morris*
That Judas, Godmar, and the three
Red running lions dismally
Grinned from his pennon, under which
In one straight line along the ditch,
They counted thirty heads.

                              So then,
While Robert turned round to his men,
She saw at once the wretched end,
And, stooping down, tried hard to rend
Her coif the wrong way from her head,
And hid her eyes; while Robert said:
" Nay, love, 'tis scarcely two to one,
At Poictiers where we made them run
So fast—why, sweet my love, good cheer,
The Gascon frontier is so near,
Nought after this."
                        But, " O," she said,
" My God ! my God ! I have to tread
The long way back without you; then
The court at Paris; those six men;
The gratings of the Chatelet;
The swift Seine on some rainy day
Like this, and people standing by,
And laughing, while my weak hands try
To recollect how strong men swim.
All this, or else a life with him,
For which I should be damned at last.
Would God that this next hour were past ! "

He answered not, but cried his cry,
" St. George for Marny ! " cheerily;

And laid his hand upon her rein.
Alas ! no man of all his train
Gave back that cheery cry again;
And, while for rage his thumb beat fast
Upon his sword-hilt, some one cast
About his neck a kerchief long,
And bound him.

           Then they went along
To Godmar; who said: " Now, Jehane,
Your lover's life is on the wane
So fast, that, if this very hour
You yield not as my paramour,
He will not see the rain leave off—
Nay, keep your tongue from gibe and scoff,
Sir Robert, or I slay you now."
She laid her hand upon her brow,
Then gazed upon the palm, as though
She thought her forehead bled, and—" No "
She said, and turned her head away,
As there were nothing else to say,
And everything were settled; red
Grew Godmar's face from chin to head:
" Jehane, on yonder hill there stands
My castle, guarding well my lands;
What hinders me from taking you,
And doing that I list to do
To your fair wilful body, while
Your knight lies dead ? "

                  A wicked smile
Wrinkled her face, her lips grew thin,
A long way out she thrust her chin:
" You know that I should strangle you
While you were sleeping; or bite through

Your throat, by God's help: ah!" she said
"Lord Jesus, pity your poor maid!
For in such wise they hem me in,
I cannot choose but sin and sin,
Whatever happens: yet I think
They could not make me eat or drink,
And so should I just reach my rest."

"Nay, if you do not my behest,
O Jehane! though I love you well,"
Said Godmar, "would I fail to tell
All that I know?" "Foul lies," she said.
"Eh? lies, my Jehane? by God's head,
At Paris folks would deem them true!
Do you know, Jehane, they cry for you,
'Jehane the brown! Jehane the brown!
Give us Jehane to burn or drown!'"
Eh—gag me Robert!—sweet my friend,
This were indeed a piteous end
For those long fingers, and long feet,
And long neck, and smooth shoulders sweet;
An end that few men would forget
That saw it. So, an hour yet:
Consider, Jehane, which to take
Of life or death!

                                    So, scarce awake,
Dismounting, did she leave that place,
And totter some yards: with her face
Turned upward to the sky she lay,
Her head on a wet heap of hay,
And fell asleep: and while she slept,
And did not dream, the minutes crept
Round to the twelve again; but she,

Being waked at last, sighed quietly,
And strangely childlike came, and said:
" I will not."   Straightway Godmar's head,
As though it hung on strong wires, turned
Most sharply round, and his face burned.

For Robert—both his eyes were dry,
He could not weep, but gloomily
He seemed to watch the rain; yea, too,
His lips were firm; he tried once more
To touch her lips; she reached out, sore
And vain desire so tortured them,
The poor grey lips, and now the hem
Of his sleeve brushed them.

                             With a start
Up Godmar rose, thrust them apart;
From Robert's throat he loosed the bands
Of silk and mail; with empty hands
Held out, she stood and gazed, and saw,
The long bright blade without a flaw
Glide out from Godmar's sheath, his hand
In Robert's hair; she saw him bend
Back Robert's head; she saw him send
The thin steel down; the blow told well,
Right backward the knight Robert fell,
And moaned as dogs do, being half dead,
        Unwitting, as I deem: so then
        Godmar turned grinning to his men,
        Who ran, some five to six, and beat
        His head to pieces at their feet,

Then Godmar turned again and said:
" So, Jehane, the first fitte is read !

Take note, my lady, that your way
Lies backward to the Chatelet ! "
She shook her head and gazed awhile
At her cold hands with a rueful smile,
As though this thing had made her mad.

This was the parting that they had
Beside the haystack in the floods

*William
Morris*

IN PRISON

Wearily, drearily,
Half the day long,
Flap the great banners
High over the stone;
Strangely and eerily
Sounds the wind's song,
Bending the banner-poles.

While, all alone,
Watching the loophole's spark,
Lie I, with life all dark,
Feet tethered, hands fettered
Fast to the stone,
The grim walls, square lettered
With prisoned men's groan.

Still strain the banner-poles
Through the wind's song,
Westward the banner rolls
Over my wrong.

*Gerard
Manley
Hopkins*

Glory be to God for dappled things—
    For skies of couple-colour as a brinded cow;
        For rose-moles all in stipple upon trout
        that swim;
Fresh-firecoal chestnut-falls; finches' wings;
    Landscape plotted and pieced—fold, fallow,
        and plough;
        And all trades, their gear and tackle and
        trim.

All things counter, original, spare, strange;
    Whatever is fickle, freckled (who knows how?)
        With swift, slow; sweet, sour; adazzle, dim;
He fathers-forth whose beauty is past change:
        Praise him.

FELIX RANDAL

Felix Randal the farrier, O he is dead then ? my
    duty all ended.
Who have watched his mould of man, big-boned
    and hardy-handsome
Pining, pining, till time when reason rambled in
    it and some
Fatal four disorders, fleshed there, all contended ?

Sickness broke him. Impatient he cursed at
    first, but mended
Being anointed and all; though a heavenlier
    heart began some

148

Months earlier, since I had our sweet reprieve *Gerard*
    and ransom   *Manley*
Tendered to him. Ah well, God rest him all *Hopkins*
    road ever he offended!

This seeing the sick endears them to us, us too
    it endears.
My tongue had taught thee comfort, touch had
    quenched thy tears,
Thy tears that touched my heart, child, Felix,
    poor Felix Randal;

How far from then forethought of, all thy more
    boisterous years,
When thou at the random grim forge, powerful
    amidst peers,
Didst fettle for the great grey drayhorse his
    bright and battering sandal!

THE HABIT OF PERFECTION

    Elected Silence, sing to me
    And beat upon my whorled ear,
    Pipe me to pastures still and be
    The music that I care to hear.

    Shape nothing, lips; be lovely-dumb:
    It is the shut, the curfew sent
    From there where all surrenders come
    Which only makes you eloquent.

Be shelled, eyes, with double dark
And find the uncreated light:
This ruck and reel which you remark
Coils, keeps and teases simple sight.

Palate, the hutch of tasty lust,
Desire not to be rinsed with wine:
The can must be so sweet, the crust
So fresh that come in fasts divine !

Nostrils, your careless breath that spend
Upon the stir and keep of pride,
What relish shall the censers send
Along the sanctuary side !

O feel-of-primrose hands, O feet
That want the yield of plushy sward,
But you shall walk the golden street,
And you unhouse and house the Lord.

And Poverty, be thou the bride
And now the marriage feast begun,
And lily-coloured clothes provide
Your spouse not laboured-at, nor spun.

SPRING AND FALL

Margaret, are you grieving
Over Goldengrove unleaving ?
Leaves like the things of man you
With your fresh thoughts care for, can you ?
Ah! as the heart grows older

It will come to such sights colder   *Gerard*
By and by, nor spare a sigh   *Manley*
Though worlds of wanwood leafmeal lie;   *Hopkins*
And yet you will weep and know why.
   Now no matter, child, the name:
Sorrow's springs are the same
Nor mouth had, no, nor mind expressed
What heart heard of, ghost guessed:
It is the blight man was born for,
It is Margaret you mourn for.

From THE WOODS OF WESTERMAIN   *George*
                                       Meredith

Enter these enchanted woods,
      You who dare.
Nothing harms beneath the leaves
More than waves a swimmer cleaves.
Toss your heart up with the lark,
Foot at peace with mouse and worm,
      Fair you fare.
Only at a dread of dark
Quaver, and they quit their form:
Thousand eyeballs under hoods
      Have you by the hair.
Enter these enchanted woods,
      You who dare.

Here the snake across your path
Stretches in his golden bath:
Mossy-footed squirrels leap
Soft as winnowing plumes of sleep:
Yaffles on a chuckle skim
Low to laugh from branches dim:

151

Up the pine, where sits the star,
Rattles deep the moth-winged jar.
Each has business of his own;
But should you distrust a tone,
    Then beware.
Shudder all the haunted roods,
All the eyeballs under hoods
    Shroud you in their glare.
Enter these enchanted woods,
    You who dare.

From MODERN LOVE

What are we first? First, animals; and next
Intelligences at a leap; on whom
Pale lies the distant shadow of the tomb,
And all that draweth on the tomb for text.
Into which state comes Love, the crowning sun:
Beneath whose light the shadow loses form.
We are the lords of life, and life is warm.
Intelligence and instinct now are one.
But nature says: " My children most they seem
When they least know me: therefore I decree
That they shall suffer."   Swift doth young Love
    flee,
And we stand wakened, shivering from our
    dream.
Then if we study Nature we are wise.
Thus do the few who live but with the day:
The scientific animals are they.—
Lady, this is my sonnet to your eyes.

FADING-LEAF AND FALLEN-LEAF

Richard Garnett

Said Fading-leaf to Fallen-leaf:—
  " I toss alone on a forsaken tree,
It rocks and cracks with every gust that racks
    Its straining bulk; say, how is it with thee ? "

Said Fallen-leaf to Fading-leaf:—
  " A heavy foot went by, an hour ago;
Crushed into clay I stain the way;
    The loud wind calls me, and I cannot go."

Said Fading-leaf to Fallen-leaf:—
  " Death lessons Life, a ghost is ever wise;
Teach me a way to live till May
    Laughs fair with fragrant lips and loving eyes."

Said Fallen-leaf to Fading-leaf:—
  "Hast loved fair eyes and lips of gentle breath?
Fade then and fall—thou hast had all
    That Life can give, ask somewhat now of
    Death."

IN THE HIGHLANDS

Robert Louis Stevenson

In the highlands, in the country places,
Where the old plain men have rosy faces,
And the young fair maidens
Quiet eyes;
Where essential silence cheers and blesses,
And for ever in the hill-recesses
Her more lovely music
Broods and dies.

Robert
Louis
Stevenson O to mount again where erst I haunted;
Where the old red hills are bird-enchanted,
And the low green meadows
Bright with sward;
And when even dies, the million-tinted,
And the night has come, and planets glinted,
Lo, the valley hollow
Lamp-bestarred!

O to dream, O to awake and wander
There, and with delight to take and render,
Through the trance of silence,
Quiet breath;
Lo! for there, among the flowers and grasses,
Only the mightier movement sounds and passes;
Only winds and rivers,
Life and death.

A PORTRAIT

I am a kind of farthing dip,
Unfriendly to the nose and eyes;
A blue-behinded ape, I skip
Upon the trees of Paradise.

At mankind's feast, I take my place
In solemn, sanctimonious state,
And have the air of saying grace
While I defile the dinner plate.

I am " the smiler with the knife,"
The battener upon garbage, I—
Dear Heaven, with such a rancid life,
Were it not better far to die?

154

Yet still, about the human pale,
I love to scamper, love to race,
To swing by my irreverent tail
All over the most holy place;

And when at length, some golden day,
The unfailing sportsman, aiming at,
Shall bag, me—all the world shall say:
Thank God, and there's an end of that!

Robert
Louis
Stevenson

REQUIEM

Under the wide and starry sky
Dig the grave and let me lie:
Glad did I live and gladly die,
   And I laid me down with a will.

This be the verse you grave for me:
Here he lies where he longed to be;
Home is the sailor, home from sea,
   And the hunter home from the hill.

CHORUS From ATALANTA IN CALYDON

Algernon
Charles
Swinburne

When the hounds of spring are on winter's
   traces,
  The mother of months in meadow or plain
Fills the shadows and windy places
  With lisp of leaves and ripple of rain;

And the brown bright nightingale amorous
Is half assuaged for Itylus,
For the Thracian ships and the foreign faces.
  The tongueless vigil, and all the pain.

Come with bows bent and with emptying of
    quivers,
  Maiden most perfect, lady of light,
With a noise of winds and many rivers,
  With a clamour of waters, and with might;
Bind on thy sandals, O thou most fleet,
Over the splendour and speed of thy feet;
For the faint east quickens, the wan west shivers,
  Round the feet of the day and the feet of the
    night.

Where shall we find her, how shall we sing to her,
  Fold our hands round her knees, and cling?
O that man's heart were as fire and could spring
    to her,
  Fire, or the strength of the streams that spring!
For the stars and the winds are unto her
As raiment, as songs of the harp-player;
For the risen stars and the fallen cling to her,
  And the southwest-wind and the west-wind
    sing.

For winter's rains and ruins are over,
  And all the season of snows and sins;
The days dividing lover and lover,
  The light that loses, the night that wins;

And time remember'd is grief forgotten,
And frosts are slain and flowers begotten,
And in green underwood and cover
   Blossom by blossom the spring begins.

*Algernon
Charles
Swinburne*

The full streams feed on flower of rushes,
   Ripe grasses trammel a travelling foot,
The faint fresh flame of the young year flushes
   From leaf to flower and flower to fruit;
And fruit and leaf are as gold and fire,
And the oat is heard above the lyre,
And the hoofed heel of a satyr crushes
   The chestnut-husk at the chestnut-root.

And Pan by noon and Bacchus by night,
   Fleeter of foot than the fleet-foot kid,
Follows with dancing and fills with delight
   The Mænad and the Bassarid;
And soft as lips that laugh and hide
The laughing leaves of the trees divide,
And screen from seeing and leave in sight
   The god pursuing, the maiden hid.

The ivy falls with the Bacchanal's hair
   Over her eyebrows hiding her eyes;
The wild vine slipping down leaves bare
   Her bright breast shortening into sighs;
The wild vine slips with the weight of its leaves,
But the berried ivy catches and cleaves
To the limbs that glitter, the feet that scare
   The wolf that follows, the fawn that flies.

Algernon
Charles
Swinburne
A FORSAKEN GARDEN

In a coign of the cliff between lowland and high-
    land,
    At the sea-down's edge between windward and
      lee,
Walled round with rocks as an inland island,
    The ghost of a garden fronts the sea.
A girdle of brushwood and thorn encloses
    The steep square slope of the blossomless bed
Where the weeds that grew green from the graves
     of its roses
        Now lie dead.

The fields fall southward, abrupt and broken,
    To the low last edge of the long lone land.
If a step should sound or a word be spoken,
    Would a ghost not rise at the strange guest's
      hand?
So long have the grey bare walks lain guestless,
    Through branches and briers if a man make
      way,
He shall find no life but the sea-wind's, restless
      Night and day.

The dense hard passage is blind and stifled
    That crawls by a track none turn to climb
To the strait waste place that the years have
    rifled
    Of all but the thorns that are touched not of
     time.
The thorns he spares when the rose is taken;
    The rocks are left when he wastes the plain.
The wind that wanders, the weeds wind-shake,
      These remain.

Not a flower to be pressed of the foot that falls *Algernon*
   not; *Charles*
  As the heart of a dead man the seed-plots *Swinburne*
   are dry;
From the thicket of thorns whence the nightin-
   gale calls not,
  Could she call, there were never a rose to
   reply.
Over the meadows that blossom and wither
  Rings but the note of a sea-bird's song;
Only the sun and the rain come hither
      All year long.

The sun burns sere and the rain dishevels
  One gaunt bleak blossom of scentless breath.
Only the wind here hovers and revels
  In a round where life seems barren as death.
Here there was laughing of old, there was
   weeping.
  Haply, of lovers none ever will know,
Whose eyes went seaward a hundred sleeping
      Years ago.

Heart handfast in heart as they stood, " Look
   thither,"
  Did he whisper? " look forth from the
   flowers to the sea;
For the foam-flowers endure when the rose-
   blossoms wither,
  And men that love lightly may die—but we ? "
And the same wind sang and the same waves
   whitened,

And or ever the garden's last petals were shed,
In the lips that had whispered, the eyes that had
    lightened,
        Love was dead.

Or they loved their life through, and then went
    whither ?
    And were one to the end; but what end who
    knows ?
Love deep as the sea as a rose must wither,
    As the rose-red seaweed that mocks the rose.
Shall the dead take thought for the dead to love
    them ?
    What love was ever as deep as a grave ?
They are loveless now as the grass above them
        Or the wave.

All are at one now, roses and lovers,
    Not known of the cliffs and the fields and the
    sea.
Not a breath of the time that has been hovers
    In the air now soft with a summer to be.
Not a breath shall there sweeten the seasons
    hereafter
    Of the flowers or the lovers that laugh now
    or weep,
When as they that are free now of weeping and
    laughter
        We shall sleep.

Here death may deal not again for ever;
    Here change may come not till all change end.
From the graves they have made they shall rise
    up never,

Who have left nought living to ravage and
    rend. *Algernon*
Earth, stones, and thorns of the wild ground *Charles*
     growing, *Swinburne*
  While the sun and the rain live, these shall be;
Till a last wind's breath upon all these blowing
       Roll the sea.

Till the slow sea rise and the sheer cliff crumble,
  Till terrace and meadow the deep gulfs drink,
Till the strength of the waves of the high tides
    humble
  The fields that lessen, the rocks that shrink,
Here now in his triumph where all things falter,
  Stretched out on the spoils that his own hand
     spread,
As a god self-slain on his own strange altar,
      Death lies dead.

"I AM THE REAPER" *W. E. Henley*

I am the Reaper.
All things with heedful hook
Silent I gather.
Pale roses touched with the spring,
Tall corn in summer,
Fruits rich with autumn, and frail winter
    blossoms—
Reaping, still reaping—
All things with heedful hook
Timely I gather.

W. E. I am the Sower.
Henley All the unbodied life
      Runs through my seed-sheet.
      Atom with atom wed,
      Each quickening the other,
      Fall through my hands, ever changing, still
          changeless.
      Ceaselessly sowing,
      Life, incorruptible life,
      Flows from my seed-sheet.

      Maker and breaker,
      I am the ebb and the flood,
      Here and Hereafter.
      Sped through the tangle and coil
      Of infinite nature,
      Viewless and soundless I fashion all being.
      Taker and giver,
      I am the womb and the grave,
      The Now and the Ever.

I. M. MARGARITAE SORORI

      A late lark twitters from the quiet skies;
      And from the west,
      Where the sun, his day's work ended,
      Lingers as in content,
      There falls on the old, grey city
      An influence luminous and serene,
      A shining peace.

The smoke ascends
In a rosy-and-golden haze.   The spires
Shine, and are changed.   In the valley
Shadows rise.   The lark sings on.   The sun,
Closing his benediction,
Sinks, and the darkening air
Thrills with a sense of the triumphing night—
Night with her train of stars
And her great gift of sleep.

So be my passing !
My task accomplished and the long day done,
My wages taken, and in my heart
Some late lark singing,
Let me be gathered to the quiet west,
The sundown splendid and serene.
Death.

*W. E.
Henley*

HÉLAS !

*Oscar
Wilde*

To drift with every passion till my soul
Is a stringed lute on which all winds can play,
Is it for this that I have given away
Mine ancient wisdom and austere control ?
Methinks my life is a twice-written scroll
Scrawled over on some boyish holiday
With idle songs for pipe and virelay
That do but mar the secret of the whole.
Surely there was a time I might have trod
The sunlit heights, and from life's dissonance
Struck one clear chord to reach the ears of God :
Is that time dead ?   Lo, with a little rod
I did but touch the honey of romance—
And must I lose a soul's inheritance ?

Wilfrid
Scawen
Blunt

He who has once been happy is for aye
    Out of destruction's reach. His fortune
    then
Holds nothing secret; and Eternity,
    Which is a mystery to other men,
Has like a woman given him its joy.
    Time is his conquest. Life, if it should
    fret,
Has paid him tribute. He can bear to die,
    He who has once been happy! When
    I set
The world before me and survey its range,
    Its mean ambitions, its scant fantasies,
The shreds of pleasure which for lack of
    change
    Men wrap around them and call happiness,
The poor delights which are the tale and sun
Of the world's courage in its martyrdom;

When I hear laughter from a tavern door,
    When I see crowds agape and in the rain
Watching on tiptoe and with stifled roar
    To see a rocket fired or a bull slain,
When misers handle gold, when orators
    Touch strong men's hearts with glory till they
      weep,
When cities deck their streets for barren wars
    Which have laid waste their youth, and when
      I keep
Calmly the count of my own life and see
    On what poor stuff my manhood's dreams
      were fed

Till I too learned what dole of vanity
  Will serve a human soul for daily bread,
—Then I remember that I once was young
And lived with Esther the world's gods among.

Wilfrid
Scawen
Blunt

THE MOCKERY OF LIFE

God ! What a mockery is this life of ours !
Cast forth in blood and pain from our mother's
    womb,
Most like an excrement, and weeping showers
Of senseless tears: unreasoning, naked, dumb,
The symbol of all weakness and the sum:
Our very life a sufferance.—Presently,
Grown stronger, we must fight for standing-
    room
Upon the earth, and the bare liberty
To breathe and move. We crave the right to
    toil.
We push, we strive, we jostle with the rest.
We learn new courage, stifle our old fears,
Stand with stiff backs, take part in every broil.
It may be that we love, that we are blest.
It may be, for a little space of years,
We conquer fate and half forget our tears.

And then fate strikes us. First our joys decay.
Youth, with its pleasures, is a tale soon told.
We grow a little poorer day by day.
Old friendships falter. Loves grow strangely
    cold.

Wilfrid　In vain we shift our hearts to a new hold
Scawen　And barter joy for joy, the less for less.
Blunt　　We doubt our strength, our wisdom, and our
　　　　　gold.
　　　We stand alone, as in a wilderness
　　　Of doubts and terrors.　Then, if we be wise,
　　　We make our terms with fate and, while we may,
　　　Sell our life's last sad remnant for a hope.
　　　And it is wisdom thus to close our eyes.
　　　But for the foolish, those who cannot pray,
　　　What else remains of their dark horoscope
　　　But a tall tree and courage and a rope ?

　　　And who shall tell what ignominy death
　　　Has yet in store for us ; what abject fears
　　　Even for the best of us ; what fights for breath ;
　　　What sobs, what supplications, what wild tears ;
　　　What impotence of soul against despairs
　　　Which blot out reason ?—The last trembling
　　　　　thought
　　　Of each poor brain, as dissolution nears,
　　　Is not of fair life lost, of Heaven bought
　　　And glory won.　'Tis not the thought of grief ;
　　　Of friends deserted ; loving hearts which bleed ;
　　　Wives, sisters, children who around us weep.
　　　But only a mad clutching for relief
　　　From physical pain, importunate Nature's
　　　　　need ;
　　　The search as for a womb where we may creep
　　　Back from the world, to hide,—perhaps to sleep.

*John
Davidson*

I felt the world a-spinning on its nave,
   I felt it sheering blindly round the sun;
I felt the time had come to find a grave:
   I knew it in my heart my days were done.
I took my staff in hand; I took the road,
And wandered out to seek my last abode.
        Hearts of gold and hearts of lead
          Sing it yet in sun and rain,
            " Heel and toe from dawn to dusk,
             Round the world and home again ".

O long before the bere was steeped for malt,
   And long before the grape was crushed for
     wine,
The glory of the march without a halt,
   The triumph of a stride like yours and mine
Was known to folk like us, who walked
    about,
To be the sprightliest cordial out and out !
        Folk like us, with hearts that beat,
          Sang it too in sun and rain—
            " Heel and toe from dawn to dusk,
             Round the world and home again ".

My feet are heavy now, but on I go,
   My head erect beneath the tragic years.
The way is steep, but I would have it so;
   And dusty, but I lay the dust with tears,
Though none can see me weep: alone I climb
The rugged path that leads me out of time—

Out of time and out of all,
  Singing yet in sun and rain,
" Heel and toe from dawn to dusk,
  Round the world and home again ".

Farewell the hope that mocked, farewell despair
  That went before me still and made the pace.
The earth is full of graves, and mine was there
  Before my life began, my resting-place;
And I shall find it out and with the dead
Lie down for ever, all my sayings said—
    Deeds all done and songs all sung,
      While others chant in sun and rain,
    " Heel and toe from dawn to dusk,
      Round the world and home again ".

From THE TESTAMENT OF A MAN FORBID

This Beauty, this Divinity, this Thought,
This hallowed bower and harvest of delight
Whose roots ethereal seemed to clutch the stars,
Whose amaranths perfumed eternity,
Is fixed in earthly soil enriched with bones
Of used-up workers; fattened with the blood
Of prostitutes, the prime manure; and dressed
With brains of madmen and the broken hearts
Of children.   Understand it, you at least
Who toil all day and writhe and groan all night
With roots of luxury, a cancer struck
In every muscle; out of you it is
Cathedrals rise and Heaven blossoms fair;
You are the hidden putrefying source
Of beauty and delight, of leisured hours,
Of passionate loves and high imaginings;
You are the dung that keeps the roses sweet.

168

" NON SUM QUALIS ERAM BONAE SUB REGNO CYNARAE "

Ernest Dowson

Last night, ah yesternight, betwixt her lips and
  mine
There fell thy shadow, Cynara ! thy breath was
  shed
Upon my soul between the kisses and the wine;
And I was desolate and sick of an old passion,
  Yea, I was desolate and bowed my head:
I have been faithful to thee, Cynara ! in my
  fashion.

All night upon mine heart I felt her warm heart
  beat,
Night-long within mine arms in love and sleep
  she lay;
Surely the kisses of her bought red mouth were
  sweet;
But I was desolate and sick of an old passion,
  When I awoke and found the dawn was grey:
I have been faithful to thee, Cynara ! in my
  fashion.

I have forgot much, Cynara ! gone with the
  wind,
Flung roses, roses riotously with the throng,
Dancing, to put thy pale, lost lilies out of mind;
But I was desolate and sick of an old passion,
  Yea, all the time, because the dance was long:
I have been faithful to thee, Cynara ! in my
  fashion.

John
Davidson

I cried for madder music and for stronger wine,
But when the feast is finished and the lamps
    expire,
Then falls thy shadow, Cynara ! the night is
    thine ;
And I am desolate and sick of an old passion,
    Yea, hungry for the lips of my desire :
I have been faithful to thee, Cynara ! in my
    fashion.

Mary
Coleridge

JEALOUSY

" The myrtle bush grew shady
    Down by the ford."—
" Is it even so ? " said my lady.
    " Even so ! " said my lord.
" The leaves are set too thick together
    For the point of a sword."

" The arras in your room hangs close,
    No light between !
You wedded one of those
    That see unseen."—
" Is it even so ? " said the King's Majesty.
    " Even so ! " said the Queen.

Thomas
Hardy

PROUD SONGSTERS

The thrushes sing as the sun is going,
And the finches whistle in ones and pairs,
And as it gets dark loud nightingales
      In bushes
Pipe, as they can when April wears,
   As if all Time were theirs.

These are brand-new birds of twelve-months'
    growing,
Which a year ago, or less than twain,
No finches were, nor nightingales,
      Nor thrushes,
But only particles of grain,
  And earth, and air, and rain.

AFTERWARDS

When the Present has latched its postern behind
    my tremulous stay,
  And the May month flaps its glad green leaves
    like wings,
Delicate-filmed as new-spun silk, will the neigh-
  bours say,
  " He was a man who used to notice such
    things " ?

If it be in the dusk when, like an eyelid's sound-
    less blink,
  The dewfall-hawk comes crossing the shades
    to alight
Upon the wind-warped upland thorn, a gazer
    may think,
  " To him this must have been a familiar
    sight."

If I pass during some nocturnal blackness, mothy
    and warm,
  When the hedgehog travels furtively over the
    lawn,

One may say, " He strove that such innocent creatures should come to no harm,
But he could do little for them; and now he is gone."

If, when hearing that I have been stilled at last, they stand at the door,
Watching the full-starred heavens that winter sees,
Will this thought rise on those who will meet my face no more,
" He was one who had an eye for such mysteries " ?

And will any say when my bell of quittance is heard in the gloom,
And a crossing breeze cuts a pause in its outrollings,
Till they rise again, as they were a new bell's boom,
" He hears it not now, but used to notice such things " ?

HEREDITY

I am the family face;
Flesh perishes, I live on,
Projecting trait and trace
Through time to times anon,
And leaping from place to place
Over oblivion.

The years-heired feature that can
In curve and voice and eye
Despise the human span
Of durance—that is I;
The eternal thing in man,
That heeds no call to die.

ON HIS EIGHTY-SIXTH BIRTHDAY

Well, World, you have kept faith with me,
    Kept faith with me;
Upon the whole you have proved to be
    Much as you said you were.
Since as a child I used to lie
Upon the leaze and watch the sky,
Never, I own, expected I
    That life would all be fair.

'Twas then you said, and since have said,
    Times since have said,
In that mysterious voice you shed
    From clouds and hills around:
" Many have loved me desperately,
Many with smooth serenity,
While some have shown contempt of me
    Till they dropped underground.

" I do not promise overmuch,
    Child; overmuch;
Just neutral-tinted haps and such,"
    You said to minds like mine.
Wise warning for your credit's sake !
Which I for one failed not to take,
And hence could stem such strain and ache
    As each year might assign.

BIOGRAPHICAL NOTES

MATTHEW ARNOLD (1822–1888). [*page* 93.] Son of Thomas Arnold, the famous headmaster of Rugby. Educated at Rugby, Winchester and Oxford, where he became a Fellow of Oriel College while Clough was a Fellow there. In 1857 Arnold was appointed to the professorship of poetry at Oxford which he held for ten years. Most of his poetry was written before 1867, after which date he concentrated his attention on criticism literary, religious and political, and the improvement of education in this country.

WILLIAM BARNES (1801–1886). [*page* 49.] Born at Rushay, Dorset. Son of a farmer. Took Holy Orders and became Rector of Carne. The majority of his poems are written in the Dorset dialect.

THOMAS LOVELL BEDDOES (1803–1849). [*page* 27.] Son of a distinguished physician and nephew of Maria Edgeworth. Educated at Charterhouse and Oxford and studied medicine on the Continent. Most of his poetry is in dramatic form, and his genius for the macabre and for violent and grotesque imagery reached its height in *Death's Jest-Book*, begun in 1825 but not published until 1850, a year after his death by suicide.

WILFRID SCAWEN BLUNT (1840–1922). [*page* 164.] Born in Sussex. Entered the Diplomatic Service. In his political writings and activities he was a violent nationalist and a vigorous advocate of Home Rule for India and Ireland, where in 1887 he was sentenced to two months' imprisonment. He published several volumes of poetry, notably *Love Sonnets of Proteus*, which appeared in 1880.

EMILY BRONTË (1818–1848). [*page* 39.] Born at Hartshead, Yorkshire, sister to Charlotte, Anne and Branwell Brontë. Her life was unhappy and uneventful. She was the author of the remarkable novel *Wuthering Heights* and of a number of poems.

Refusing to see a doctor until too late, she died of tuberculosis at the age of thirty at Haworth near Bradford.

ELIZABETH BARRETT BROWNING (1806–1861). [*page* 41.] Born at Coxhoe Hall, Durham. Daughter of Edward Barrett Moulton Barrett. Her health was always delicate but did not prevent her literary activity, and she was an established and popular poet at the time of her romantic marriage with Robert Browning in 1846. From that time until her death she lived with her husband in Italy.

ROBERT BROWNING (1812–1889). [*page* 81.] Born in Camberwell. Son of a senior clerk in Bank of England. Educated by a tutor and at University College, London. *Pauline* appeared anonymously and unnoticed in 1833, but *Paracelsus*, published in 1835, attracted the attention of Carlyle and Wordsworth. *Strafford, Sordello* and other volumes followed, but when in 1846 he married Elizabeth Barrett the quality of his poetry was still unrecognised outside a small circle. After his marriage until his wife's death in 1861 he was with her in Italy, where he wrote *Men and Women.* Subsequently he divided his time between Italy and England, and published *The Ring and the Book* and about a dozen other volumes of poetry, of which the last, *Asolando,* appeared on the day of his death. Like his great contemporary, Tennyson, who was born three years before him and survived him for three years, he was buried in Westminster Abbey.

THOMAS CARLYLE (1795–1881). [*page* 43.] Born at Ecclefechan in Dumfriesshire. Son of a stonemason. Chiefly famous as a historian and essayist who exercised a profound influence on Victorian thought. Although at his death burial in Westminster Abbey was offered, Carlyle was buried with his own people in accordance with instructions he had left.

JOHN CLARE (1793–1864). [*page* 36.] Born at Helpstone near Peterborough. Son of a crippled labourer. Became a herd-boy, militiaman and vagrant. A Stamford bookseller helped him to have his first book of poems published in 1820. This attracted the attention of several noblemen who set Clare up in a farm. He failed as a farmer and in 1837 he became insane. The later years of his life were spent in Northampton Asylum, where some of his best poetry was written.

ARTHUR HUGH CLOUGH (1819–1861). [*page* 44.] Son of a cotton merchant in Liverpool. Educated at Rugby and Oxford, where as a Fellow of Oriel College he came under the influence of Newman. He subsequently became a sceptic, threw up his Fellowship and after a period as Principal of University Hall, London, was appointed an examiner in the Education Office. He died at Florence.

MARY ELIZABETH COLERIDGE (1861–1907). [*page* 170.] Great-niece of Samuel Taylor Coleridge. Author of two novels and of several volumes of poetry which she published anonymously.

HARTLEY COLERIDGE (1796–1849). [*page* 23.] Born at Clevedon. Eldest son of Samuel Taylor Coleridge. Spent his early years at Keswick with the Lake poets and in 1815 was sent to Oxford at Southey's expense. He became a probationer Fellow of Oriel College, but in 1820 was dismissed for intemperance. He then started a school at Ambleside, but this failed and most of the last twenty years of his life were spent in seclusion at Grasmere.

WILLIAM JOHNSON CORY (1823–1892). [*page* 125.] Educated at Eton where he subsequently became an Assistant Master. Author of a number of educational works, and of two volumes of poems of which his best known is his translation of the Epitaph on Heraclitus by Callimachus.

JOHN DAVIDSON (1857–1909). [*page* 167.] Born at Barrhead, Renfrewshire. Son of a Dissenting Minister. Schoolmaster in Scotland until 1889, when he settled in London and published various plays and volumes of verse. He died in circumstances that suggested suicide.

LORD DE TABLEY (1835–1895). [*page* 132.] John Byrne Leicester Warren, later Baron de Tabley. Educated at Eton and Christ Church, Oxford. For a time attached to the

British Embassy in Constantinople. Studied botany. Published several volumes of verse pseudonymously before in 1893 and 1895 publishing over his own name two series of *Poems Dramatic and Lyrical*.

SYDNEY THOMPSON DOBELL (1824–1874). [*page* 57.] Born at Cranbrook, Kent. Son of a wine merchant. His first work, *The Roman*, was published in 1850 and was well received. *Balder*, *Sonnets on the War*, and other volumes of verse followed. Dobell was a prominent member of what was known as the " Spasmodic School " of poetry.

ERNEST DOWSON (1867–1900). [*page* 169.] Born at Lee in Kent. Father was owner of a small dock in Limehouse. Short time at Queen's College, Oxford. Became member of Café Royal group of writers. Published two volumes of poetry, *Verses* and *Decorations*. Died in poverty of tuberculosis.

RALPH WALDO EMERSON (1803–1882). [*page* 45.] Born in Concord, Mass. Educated at Harvard, studied theology, became a pastor at Boston, resigned owing to religious doubts. Visited Europe and met Coleridge, Wordsworth and Carlyle. On his return to America he lectured on literature, history and cultural subjects generally and acquired a wide reputation as an idealist thinker, essayist and poet.

EDWARD FITZGERALD (1809–1883). [*page* 54.] Born near Woodbridge, Suffolk. Educated at Bury St. Edmunds and Trinity College, Cambridge. Subsequently lived quietly in East Anglia, where he wrote several minor biographies and semi-academic works and a number of translations from the Greek and Spanish. His claim to fame rests on his English poetic version of the *Rubáiyát of Omar Khayyám*. He was also one of the most graceful exponents of the art of letter-writing.

RICHARD GARNETT (1835–1906). [*page* 153.] Born at Lichfield. Son of Assistant Keeper of Printed Books at the British Museum. Educated at a school in Bloomsbury. For fifty years associated with the British Museum Library, rising from the position of an assistant librarian to that of Keeper of Printed Books. Garnett was a man of great erudition in literary matters, translated works from half-a-dozen languages and was the author of many critical books and essays, several biographies and a large number of poems.

DAVID GRAY (1838–1861). [*page* 61.] Son of a Dumbarton-shire weaver. Educated at Glasgow University, where he paid his fees by teaching. While still a youth he developed tuberculosis and, apart from his longest work, *The Luggie*, most of his poetry is a record of melancholy anticipation of early death.

THOMAS HARDY (1840–1928). [*page* 170.] Born at Upper Bockhampton near Dorchester. Son of a builder. Began as an architect but turned to literature. His first novel, *Desperate Remedies*, appeared in 1871, and was followed a year later by *Under the Greenwood Tree*. Further novels consolidated his success and popularity, but the mixed reception accorded *Jude the Obscure* in 1896 drove Hardy to poetry. *Wessex Poems* was published in 1898, the epic-drama, *The Dynasts*, in three parts, in 1903, 1906, and 1908, and various volumes of shorter poems between 1902 and 1928 when *Winter Words* appeared shortly after Hardy's death.

WILLIAM ERNEST HENLEY (1849–1903). [*page* 161.] Born at Gloucester. Crippled from childhood. Edited several periodicals and collaborated on several occasions with his friend, R. L. Stevenson. Published various volumes of poetry, several anthologies and critical works and was joint compiler of the *Slang Dictionary*.

THOMAS HOOD (1799–1845). [*page* 13.] Born in London, son of a bookseller. After a scanty education he worked for a short time in a mercantile office. Leaving there, he was employed as an engraver by an uncle. At the age of 22 he became sub-editor of the *London Magazine*, and came into contact with Lamb, Hazlitt, De Quincey and other leading writers of the time. He edited a number of periodicals and published volumes of comic and serious verse. In 1824 he married and the subsequent story of his life is one of a long and courageous struggle with poverty, ill health and adversity. It is perhaps his greatest misfortune that his talents as a humorous writer and as an author of verses with an obvious popular appeal, such as *The Song of the Shirt* and *I Remember, I Remember*, have been allowed to overshadow his importance as a serious and sometimes great poet.

GERARD MANLEY HOPKINS (1844–1889). [*page* 148.] Educated at Highgate School and Balliol College, Oxford, where he became a friend of Robert Bridges. In 1866 was converted to the Church of Rome and two years later entered the Jesuit novitiate. In 1884 he was appointed to the chair of Greek at Dublin University. None of his poems was published during his lifetime but were collected by Bridges after his death, and it is curious that his influence on the poetry of the present day is greater than that of Bridges himself. He was responsible for the fashion of " sprung rhythm," in which stress and not syllable is counted, with the result that unpoetic words may be used in poetry without pedestrianism.

JAMES HENRY LEIGH HUNT (1794–1859). [*page* 21.] Born at Southgate and educated at Christ's Hospital. In 1813 he was sentenced to a fine of £500 and two years' imprisonment for remarks he had made about the Prince Regent in the *Examiner*, of which he was Editor. He was a friend of Byron, Moore and Lamb, and it was in the pages of the *Examiner* that Shelley and Keats were first introduced to the public. Leigh Hunt's fame rests primarily on his essays and on his contributions to literary criticism.

HENRY WADSWORTH LONGFELLOW (1807–1882). [*page* 49.] Born at Portland, Maine. Son of a lawyer. Became Professor of Modern Languages at Bowdoin, and later at Harvard. He was a prolific composer of popular verse and is known to every schoolchild as the author of *Hiawatha*, *The Courtship of Miles Standish*, and such shorter pieces as *The Village Blacksmith* and *The Wreck of the Hesperus*.

GEORGE MEREDITH (1828–1909). [*page* 151.] Born at Portsmouth. Son of a naval outfitter. Educated at Portsmouth and the Moravian School at Neuwied in Germany. Articled to a solicitor in London but abandoned law for journalism. Married at age of 21 Mary Ellen Nicolls, a widowed daughter of Thomas Love Peacock. She subsequently deserted him and died in 1861. *Modern Love* was published in 1862. In 1864 he married for the second time, and in 1866 he was the *Morning Post's* war correspondent in Italy. On the death of Tennyson in 1892 he became President of the Society of Authors and in 1905 received the Order of Merit.

WILLIAM MORRIS (1834–1896). [*page* 139.] Born at Walthamstow. Educated at Marlborough and Exeter College, Oxford. Distinguished as a poet, artist, decorator (exercising a profound influence on public taste in interior decoration), printer and socialist. His *Defence of Guenevere* was published in 1858, his *Life and Death of Jason* in 1867 and his *Earthly Paradise* in 1868–70. In 1877 he founded the Society for the Protection of Ancient Buildings. Later in 1888 and 1891 he published socialist propaganda in romance form under the titles *The Dream of John Ball* and *News from Nowhere*. Also in 1890 he started at Hammersmith the Kelmscott Press, for which he designed the type.

ARTHUR WILLIAM EDGAR O'SHAUGHNESSY (1844–1881). [*page* 130.] Born in London. Was employed first in the library and then in the natural history department of the British Museum, where he became an authority on fishes and reptiles. He published a number of volumes of verse, notably *Epic of Women* and *Music and Moonlight*, and was closely associated with Rossetti and the other pre-Raphaelites.

COVENTRY KERSEY DIGHTON PATMORE (1823–1896). [*page* 126.] Born at Woodford, Essex. Assistant in printed-book department of British Museum. Friend of Tennyson and Ruskin and contributor to the pre-Raphaelite organ *The Germ*. Author of numerous books of verse, including *The Angel in the House*, in which he celebrated married love, *The Unknown Eros* and *Amelia*.

THOMAS LOVE PEACOCK (1785–1866). [*page* 25.] Born at Weymouth. Son of a London merchant. Although mainly self-educated he acquired considerable erudition which, coupled with his keen sense of the ridiculous, gave a unique quality to his satirical romances. His verse is less interesting, except for certain songs with which he interspersed his prose works. For the greater part of his life Peacock was employed in the India Office. He was one of Shelley's closest friends and his executor. His daughter was George Meredith's first wife.

EDGAR ALLAN POE (1809–1849). [*page* 33.] Born at Boston, Mass. Parents, who were actors, died when he was a child, and Poe was brought up by a tobacco exporter to whom he subsequently showed little gratitude. He was sent to school at Stoke Newington in England and then to the University of Virginia. After a short term in the American Army, he edited various periodicals. Throughout his life he was intemperate in his habits and his death from brain fever in hospital at Baltimore followed a violent drinking bout. Although Poe was greatly esteemed as a poet, and in *The Raven* produced one of the most popular poems of the 19th century, it is as a storyteller of remarkable talent and as the originator of the detective story that he is now chiefly memorable.

CHRISTINA GEORGINA ROSSETTI (1830–1894). [*page* 127.] Sister of Dante Gabriel Rossetti. Contributed to *The Germ* under the pseudonym " Ellen Alleyne." Her *Goblin Market* appeared in 1862. She subsequently published other books of poems, mainly religious and for the most part melancholy in character.

DANTE GABRIEL ROSSETTI (1828–1882). [*page* 107.] Son of Gabriele Rossetti, an Italian patriot who came to England in 1824. Educated at King's College, London. With Holman Hunt, Millais and others founded the pre-Raphaelite Brotherhood. At first known primarily as a painter, soon established reputation as a poet by publication of *The Blessed Damozel* and other poems in *The Germ*. When his wife died in 1862 after two years of married life, Rossetti buried the MSS. of a number of his poems with her. These were exhumed later and published in 1870. Towards the end of his life Rossetti became a semi-invalid recluse, but continued to write poetry, his last book, *Ballads and Sonnets*, being published the year before he died.

WILLIAM BELL SCOTT (1811–1890). [*page* 61.] Born in Edinburgh. Son of an engraver. Friend of Rossetti and Swinburne. Painter of historical subjects and author of a life of Dürer and of several volumes of poetry.

ROBERT LOUIS STEVENSON (1850–1894). [*page* 153.] Born at Edinburgh. Son of a civil engineer. Studied engineering at Edinburgh University, but switched to law and in 1875 was called to Scottish Bar. He did not practise, however, and on account of a lung affection spent much time abroad. His first book, *An Inland Voyage*, was published in 1878. *Travels with a Donkey* appeared a year later. In 1880 he married Mrs. Osbourne in California, and in 1890 he settled with his wife and stepson, who collaborated with him in some of his later work, in Samoa, where four years later he died.

ALGERNON CHARLES SWINBURNE (1837–1909). [*page* 155.] Born in London. Son of an Admiral. Educated in France, at Eton and at Balliol College, Oxford. Published two plays when aged 24, and after visiting Italy and becoming friendly with Landor returned to England and lived for some time with Rossetti in Chelsea. *Atalanta in Calydon* appeared in 1865 and *Poems and Ballads* the following year. *Songs before Sunrise* was published in 1871. For the last thirty years of his life Swinburne lived with Theodore Watts-Dunton in Putney.

ALFRED, LORD TENNYSON (1809–1892). [*page* 66.] Born at Somersby, Lincolnshire. Son of the Rector of Somersby. Educated at Louth Grammar School and Trinity College, Cambridge, where his friends included Monckton Miles (later Lord Houghton) and Arthur Hallam whose death he was subsequently to commemorate in *In Memoriam*. While at Cambridge he won the Chancellor's Medal with a poem *Timbuctoo*, and when 21 he published his first volume of poems, which met with an indifferent reception, as did a further volume two years later. In 1833 he became engaged to Emily Sellwood, but the marriage did not take place until 1850. Meanwhile a further two-volume edition of poems and the publication of *The Princess* gave him recognition as the leading poet of his time and in the year of his marriage he became Wordsworth's successor as Poet Laureate   The same year saw the publication of *In Memoriam* which had taken him seventeen years to write. *Maud*, *The Idylls of the King* and *Enoch Arden* followed, and Tennyson then produced a series of verse dramas, publishing at the same time further volumes of poetry, of which *The Death of Œnone* was the last, appearing in the year of his death.   In 1884 Tennyson was created a Baron and shortly afterwards became the first President of the newly founded Society of Authors.   He was buried in Westminster Abbey.

JAMES THOMSON (1834–1882).   [*page* 122.]   Born at Port Glasgow.   Child of poor parents.   Was for some time an army schoolmaster, but discharged for breach of discipline in 1862.   Friend of Charles Bradlaugh, wrote for the *National Reformer* and took active part in free-thought movement.   He was the author of a number of poems of which the most important was *The City of Dreadful Night*, a remarkable record of atheistic despair.   Depression followed by dipsomania led to his death in University College Hospital.

WALT WHITMAN (1819–1892).   [*page* 115.]   Born in Long Island, New York.   Son of a farmer.   Educated at Brooklyn, entered a printing office at age of 13 and when 21 was editor of a newspaper.   In 1855 he published *Leaves of Grass*, which was violently acclaimed and as violently condemned. Whitman himself described the poems of which the book consisted as being saturated with the vehemence of pride and audacity of freedom necessary to loosen the mind of still-to-be-formed America from the folds, the superstitions, and all the long, tenacious and stifling anti-democratic authorities of Asiatic and European past.   In the Civil War Whitman helped to tend the wounded, after which he published further books of poetry and held various Government clerkships until in 1873 he had a stroke. In his later years he lived at Camden, New Jersey.

OSCAR FINGAL O'FLAHERTY WILLS WILDE (1856–1900).   [*page* 163.]   Born at Dublin.   Son of Sir William Wilde, a well-known surgeon. Educated at Trinity College, Dublin, and at Magdalen College, Oxford, where he founded an æsthetic cult. His first publication was a volume of poems which appeared in 1881. This was followed by a number of books and plays. In 1895 he was imprisoned, and while in prison wrote his famous *Ballad of Reading Gaol*. His last years were spent in obscurity in France.

INDEX OF FIRST LINES

THE PENGUIN SHAKESPEARE

EDITED BY G. B. HARRISON

PENGUIN ILLUSTRATED CLASSICS

ART DIRECTOR: ROBERT GIBBINGS

PLAYS

BACK TO METHUSELAH
BERNARD SHAW
[200]

The first dramatic work of the world's most famous living dramatist to be published at sixpence, a work which the author considers his greatest, complete with the entire text of the play and the thirty-thousand-word preface.

FOUR PLAYS
A. A. MILNE
[196]

A few plays can be as enjoyably read as seen; these four plays by A. A. Milne—*To Have the Honour, Belinda, The Dover Road* and *Mr. Pim Passes By*—possess that gracious quality.

SEVEN FAMOUS ONE-ACT PLAYS
[117]
Containing

A Marriage Has Been Arranged............*Alfred Sutro*
The Cloak..*Clifford Bax*
Two Gentlemen of Soho..................*A. P. Herbert*
Campbell of Kilmohr......................*J. A. Ferguson*
The Maker of Dreams....................*Oliphant Down*
The Dear Departed .... *Stanley Houghton*
The Monkey's Paw........................*W. W. Jacobs*

Penguin Short Stories

and

PENGUIN PARADE

SEVEN VOLUMES

NEW STORIES, POEMS, ETC., BY CONTEMPORARY WRITERS

Write and tell them

with a Penguin Pen

THE PENGUIN PEN

is a precision-made Fountain Pen fitted with an Iridium-tipped 14-carat Solid Gold Nib (Fine, Medium, or Broad).

The Ebony Streamline Holder, highly polished and unbreak-able, embodies the latest design in safety screw caps which automatically shuts off the flow of ink when in the pocket.

Self-filling, Large Ink Capacity, improved ladder feed ensures an equable and controlled ink flow.

Guaranteed for five years

BRITISH MADE THROUGHOUT